PLAY, LEARN, AND ENJOY!

A Self-Regulation Curriculum For Children

Elena A. Savina, Lindsay M. Anmuth, Kelly C. Atwood, Whitney R. Giesing, Virginia G. Larsen

Illustrated by Joshua See

RESEARCH PRESS
PUBLISHERS

2612 North Mattis Avenue, Champaign, Illinois 61822
800.519.2707 / researchpress.com

RESEARCH PRESS
PUBLISHERS

PDF versions of the forms and worksheets included in this book are available for download on the book webpage at www.researchpress.com/downloads

Copies of this book may be ordered from Research Press at the address given on the title page.

Graphic Design: Joshua See
Sound Design: David Cottrell

Cover design by McKenzie Wagner, Inc.
Printed by McNaughton & Gunn

ISBN 978-0-87822-716-7
Library of Congress Control Number 2018933627

Table of Contents

Session 2: Riverboat Trip—Day 1   33

Session 3: Riverboat Trip—Day 2   39

Session 4: Rainforest Trip—Day 1   45

All of the worksheets can be found in the Appendix for photocopying. They are also available as a free download from the *Play, Learn, and Enjoy!* book page on www.researchpress.com.

Introduction

Curriculum Overview

Play, Learn, and Enjoy! is a game-based socio-emotional learning curriculum for elementary school children. It is designed in a thematic format where children, together with stories' characters, go on imaginary adventures into the wilderness. They "travel" to mountains, a desert, a rainforest, and the Arctic; they take a riverboat trip, go ocean sailing and snorkeling. The PLE games and activities are contextual, imaginative, experiential, and collaborative. The curriculum consists of 15 one-hour sessions designed for a group of three to six children, ages six to eight. It can be implemented in various settings, including skill-building groups in schools, after-school programs, summer camps including adventure camps, and residential treatment programs. School counselors, psychologists, and occupational therapists can lead the curriculum.

A growing body of research indicates an intrinsic relationship between self-regulation and social-emotional competence, which calls for their integration in intervention and prevention programs (Riggs, Jahromi, Razza, Dillworth-Bart, & Mueller, 2006). The PLE curriculum trains children across a broad range of self-regulation skills, including neurocognitive functions (voluntary attention, working memory, and inhibition), strategic skills (time-management, planning, and organization), and emotion regulation. Self-regulation skills are trained in conjunction with social skills such as active communication, self-awareness, and collaboration with others.

The curriculum bridges a neurocognitive perspective on self-regulation with the Vygotskian framework. The neurocognitive perspective was used to map the discrete self-regulation skills (e.g., inhibition, working, memory, attention, etc.), while Vygotskian theory provided guidelines to design curriculum activities. More specifically, the curriculum puts a strong emphasis on collaborative activities and games as a developmentally appropriate context for advancing self-regulation skills in elementary school children. It further stresses the essential role of language and other external signs for self-regulation.

Definition and Outcomes of Self-Regulation

Self-regulation is defined as "the ability to comply with request, to initiate and cease activities according to situational demands, to modulate intensity, frequency and duration of verbal and motor acts…and to postpone acting upon a desired object or goal, and to generate socially approved behavior in the absence of external monitors" (Kopp, 1982, p. 199). The cognitive neuroscience framework uses the term "executive function" to describe the processes involved in self-regulation (Blair, 2002). Such processes include working memory, attention, and inhibition, which work together for planning and executing goal-directed behavior.

Self-regulation skills are essential for many domains of child functioning, including school readiness, academic success, social relationships, and mental health (McClelland, Acock, & Morrison, 2006; Lengua, 2003; Liew, 2012). A study that followed over 1,000 children from birth to adulthood found that those who exhibited stronger self-regulation skills were better off mentally and financially (Moffitt et al., 2011). Self-regulation skills undergo significant development during preschool age, coinciding with a rapid growth of the prefrontal cortex (Blair, 2002). When children enter school, the demands for self-regulation exponentially increase as they have to pay attention to their teachers, stay on task, inhibit their impulses, and regulate emotional reactions associated with frustration and disappointment. Children with self-regulation difficulties might struggle with learning and often have behavioral problems and conflicts with teachers (Berry, 2012; Lengua, 2003).

Situations That Require Self-Regulation

Children have to follow directions given by adults. Such instructions can be very simple (e.g., "Go clean your room") or complex (e.g., "Read the paragraph, highlight unfamiliar words, and find their meanings in a dictionary"). Children have to hold directions in their working memory. In addition, they need the ability to inhibit potential distractions while performing a task. For example, consider a child who is completing a math assignment while his peer attempts to distract him by making funny faces. In order to be successful, the child must block out the distraction and focus his attention on the task.

Following directions may be difficult if the child has to do something that he or she does not want to do. In such situations, task initiation and self-motivation are important. For example, a common dilemma occurs when a child would rather play with her friends than complete her homework. In this case, good self-regulation skills allow the child to recognize that if she completes her homework now, she will have more time to play with her friends later. For a child who is already engaged in a fun task (e.g., watching cartoons), self-regulation is required in order to switch to a more mundane or undesirable task, such as completing chores. Self-regulation is also necessary for children to delay the gratification of their immediate needs. For example, a child needs to wait for dinner rather than satisfy his hunger with snacks. Similarly, he needs to finish homework before playing a favorite game. Impulse control allows children to ask for what they want rather than take it from others and to inhibit their desire to shout out an answer and instead raise a hand.

In the classroom, children have to manage many activities. For this reason, time management and organization skills are essential. When children are given an assignment, they must consider the task demands and plan how to perform the task. They have to prioritize their tasks, focus on what is most important, and postpone tasks that can be completed later. Successful social interactions also require good self-regulation skills. Children need to take turns when talking to others, which requires inhibition of their immediate response. Similarly, they have to put their immediate needs aside and consider others while playing games, having conversations, and collaborating with peers on projects. Finally, children encounter many emotionally laden situations. For instance, they may feel frustrated when facing a difficult task, become anxious about an upcoming test, feel angry when being told that they cannot play, or feel sad when losing a friendship. Emotion-regulation skills allow children to manage effectively their emotional experiences.

Below is a detailed description of self-regulation skills trained in the PLE curriculum with a review of relevant research.

Neurocognitive Self-Regulation Functions

Inhibition

Inhibition is essential for self-regulation and involves the ability to suppress inappropriate responses while performing a goal-oriented behavior (Barkley, 1997; Hoffman, Schmeichel & Baddeley, 2012). There are two types of inhibition: motor and cognitive. *Motor inhibition* is necessary when the child needs to stop a habitual but irrelevant-to-the-task response, or to stop and correct himself when making an error. Motor inhibition is also important when the child is required to slow down when running in the hallway or needs to withhold a desire to hit a peer in response to an altercation. The ability to inhibit impulsive behavior is important for mental health, and children who do not do it successfully are more likely to have externalizing problems (Lengua, 2003). Impulsive children also often get in trouble, respond before thinking, make careless mistakes, and interrupt others. They also have conflicts with their teachers, which can compromise their learning (Berry, 2012). The good news is that motor inhibition can be trained through playing children's playground games such as Red Light, Green Light and Simon Says (Savina, Savenkova, & Shekotihina, 2017; Tominey & McClelland, 2011; Zhao, Chen, Fu, & Maes, 2015).

Cognitive inhibition (also called *interference control*) is involved in blocking out interfering stimuli whether they are external (e.g., noise) or internal (e.g., thoughts) (Barkley, 1998). This ability is important to keep the goal of a task in mind and combat distractions. It is related to working memory, which will we discuss in a later section.

Voluntary Attention

At any given moment, children are exposed to many stimuli: the teacher explaining the lesson, the sound of a car passing by, peers talking nearby, a dog playing outside, a shiny object on the wall, the feel of clothes against the skin, thoughts about upcoming lunch, or sadness about an earlier argument with a friend. However, not all information reaches their awareness. Attention skills allow children to "tune out" irrelevant information and focus on information that is important to the task. *Attention* refers to the ability to focus on given stimuli, while ignoring irrelevant information (Miller, 2013). Research demonstrates that children with good attention skills and task persistence at age four are likely to complete college by age 25 (McClelland, Acock, Piccinin, Rhea, & Stallings, 2013). Attention skills are also central to self-awareness, a key component of emotional intelligence (Goleman, 2013).

Attention is multifaceted and includes several modes, such as selective, sustained, divided and attentional switch (Lane, 2012). *Selective attention* allows focusing on a particular object or stimulus, while *divided attention* is involved when the child needs to attend to more than one object at the same time (Lane, 2012). *Sustained attention* permits children to maintain focus on an object for a certain amount of time and is necessary to stay on task (Lane, 2012). *Attention switching* is involved when the child needs to change the focus of attention: for example, when moving from one task to another (Miller, 2013). Research shows that attention is responsive to intervention. For example, in several studies, children with ADHD improved their attention skills after training on visual and auditory attention tasks (Semrud-Clikeman, Nielsen, Clinton, Leihua, Parle, & Connor, 1999; Tamm et al., 2016).

Working Memory

Many activities require from children an ability to hold a goal of activity in mind along with the steps that they need to follow. This ability is called *working memory*, which is a mental workspace where we temporarily store and process information (Baddeley, 2007). Working memory consists of three main components: the phonological loop, visual-spatial sketchpad, and central executive (Baddeley, 2007). The *phonological loop* temporarily stores auditory/verbal information (e.g., what is being said or read); the *visual-spatial sketchpad* stores visual information (what is being seen); and the *central executive* works to inhibit irrelevant information and allocate mental resources to a task. Research demonstrates that children with better working memory are more successful in math and reading (Bull, Espy, & Wiebe, 2008). Working memory is also important for emotion regulation (Schmeichel & Demaree, 2010). Several studies indicate that working memory can be trained, and such training leads to improvement in not only working memory but also attention control and reasoning skills (Wass, Scerif, & Johnson, 2012).

Strategic Self-Regulation Skills

To be successful in school, children need strategic self-regulation skills such as planning, prioritizing, organization, and time management. "Planning is the deliberate organization or a sequence of actions oriented towards accomplishing a specific goal...For a plan to be effective, the planner needs to be able to devise and coordinate a sequence of actions aimed at achieving a goal, as well as monitor the effectiveness of the actions for reaching the goal as the plan is executed" (Gauvain, 1992, p. 378). Planning is necessary for academic tasks (e.g., solving a math problem or writing a paper) and everyday activities (e.g., planning a party or a trip). Planning usually involves three steps: detecting a problem to be solved, anticipating steps involved in solving the problem, and sequencing out and executing those steps (Scholnick & Friedman, 1987). Planning requires working memory in order to remember the steps that need to be completed. It also involves interference control to shield out irrelevant information.

Time management is important for both academic performance and personal life. We manage time by setting goals, prioritizing, and becoming organized. Time management involves the ability to remember tasks that one needs to perform, take into account the amount of time needed for task completion, and manage progress towards those tasks (Francis-Smythe, 2006). Children are often aware of their poor organization and time-management skills and of the difficulty in completing their homework (Zentall, Harper, & Stormont-Spurgin, 1993). Research informs us that strategic skills are responsive to intervention. In one study, after participating in an eight-week after-school intervention program, children with ADHD significantly improved their time-management skills, including planning for tests, quizzes, and projects (Graham, Langberg, & Epstein, 2008).

Socio-Emotional Skills

Emotion Regulation

Children face many emotion-laden situations; therefore, they need good emotion regulation skills. Such skills are especially tested when children experience intense emotions such as being frustrated with a task, angry with parents or peers, or sad about losing a game. Emotion regulation involves physiological, attentional, cognitive, and behavioral processes aimed at initiation, modulation, or inhibition of emotional states and behaviors associated with them (Eisenberg & Spinrad, 2004). Having good emotion regulation is essential for children's mental health and academic success. Research studies demonstrate that children with good emotion regulation skills are more socially competent, have more positive interactions with others, and have better grades (Graziano, Reavis, Keane, & Calkins, 2007; Gumora & Arsenio, 2002; Denham et al., 2003; Eisenberg, Fabes, Guthrie, & Reiser, 2000). On the other hand, difficulty with regulating emotions is associated with emotional and behavioral problems and peer rejection (Eisengerg et al., 2009; Hubbard, 2001; Röll, Koglin, & Petermann, 2012). Furthermore, unregulated negative emotions can significantly disrupt children's memory and attention, thereby compromising their ability to learn (Linnenbrick & Pintrich, 2000).

Emotion regulation strategies include sharing emotional experiences with others, focusing on positive experiences, reappraising a situation to change its emotional meaning, and using deep breathing, relaxation, and mindfulness to change the emotion directly (Gross, 2002). Language is an important tool for emotion regulation. Using emotion words, such as *angry* or *sad*, children can label their emotions, reflect on their emotional experiences, and share emotional experiences with others in order to receive help (Saarni, 1999).

Social Skills

Social skills involve a broad variety of skills, including an ability to communicate, collaborate, and understand others' perspectives (Merrell & Gimpel, 1998). Children use communication skills to express their needs, establish relationships with others, and hold a conversation. In order to hold a conversation, a child must know how to approach others, choose a topic of conversation, listen, take others' perspectives, and take turns. Communication skills further include an ability to listen effectively to others. Children need effective communication skills in order to express their needs, gather information, and relate to others. Children also need to understand and use non-verbal behaviors, such as making eye contact, orienting their bodies toward others, nodding, and appropriate gesturing. Some children might find it difficult to wait their turn, keep with a particular topic of conversation, or take others' perspectives. Those who do not master communication skills are at risk of being rejected by peers and, as a result, might experience anxiety and depression (Merrell & Gimpel, 1998).

Perspective taking is an essential social skill that involves understanding other people's intentions, feelings, and thoughts (Carlo, 2006). While some children may be good at understanding how other people feel and think, they may have difficulty coordinating others' needs and feelings with their own actions (Selman, 2003). Therefore, in addition to perspective-taking ability, children need perspective coordination ability. This ability allows children to move from cooperation that is based on self-interest to collaboration, which takes into account mutual interests. In other words, perspective coordination ability involves thinking in terms of "we" rather in terms of "I" (Selman, 2003).

The Role of Language in Self-Regulation

Language is essential for self-regulation because it allows children to reflect upon and plan their behavior. Luria called language "the chief mechanism of voluntary action" (1960, p. 139). Vygotsky (1997) asserted that verbal self-regulation develops from external speech, which gradually becomes transformed into inner speech or self-talk. However, inner speech does not develop directly from external speech; there is an intermediate step called "private speech," which is observed when a child talks to himself as he or she performs a task. Thus, the child uses private speech not for communication purposes but for planning, self-guidance, and self-regulation (Berk & Potts, 1991; Vygotsky, 1997). Eventually, private speech goes inward and becomes an internalized self-regulation tool. The internalization of private speech increases children's attentional and behavioral control (Bivens & Berk, 1990). Further, children who use private speech for self-motivation and self-correction (e.g., "I can do it!", "This is not right!") show greater ability to persist on task and work independently (Chiu & Alexander, 2000).

It is important to keep in mind that we cannot teach verbal self-regulation directly through modeling and imitation. Verbal self-regulation has its origin in children's interactions with adults and peers during a collaborative activity, which may involve planning, decision-making, and problem solving (Krafft & Berk, 1998; Vygotsky, 1987). Such activities should facilitate rich verbal exchanges among children aimed at goal setting, planning, and negotiating. When internalized, verbal exchanges become a self-talk that children use to regulate themselves. Scaffolding children during collaborative activities is essential for the development of verbal self-regulation (Winsler, Diaz, & Montero, 1997). Scaffolding involves guiding of children's work and asking nondirective questions to facilitate problem solving. Scaffolding should be sensitive to children's performance and incrementally withdrawn as children learn to work independently.

Activities That Promote Self-Regulation

Play

Play is a great context for advancing children's social skills, problem-solving ability, moral reasoning, and self-regulation skills (Galyer & Evans, 2001; Newton & Jenvey, 2011; Schaefer & Reid, 2001; Piaget, 1962; Pellegrini & Gustafson, 2005; Vygotsky, 1978). Play and games are often used in therapy, as they ease the rapport between a therapist and a child and provide an avenue for children to process their socio-emotional difficulties (Schaefer & Reid, 2001; Swank, 2008).

As children develop, so does their play. Play progresses from pretend play, which is prevalent in children ages four to six, to games with rules, which begin to take place when children become older (Piaget, 1962; Vygotsky, 1978). Compared to pretend play, games place more demands on children's cognitive abilities and self-regulation, as they are more goal-directed and put more constraints on children's behavior (Piaget, 1962; Schaefer & Reid, 2001). Games are a natural medium where children learn rules (Schaefer & Reid, 2001). While playing games, children observe whether other children follow rules. Regulating peers' behavior is an important step in the development of children's own self-regulation. In addition, games may have a positive effect on children's social skills and relationships with peers.

Playing games promotes frustration tolerance and persistence because children have to accept limits on their behavior, take turns, and follow rules (Schaefer & Reid, 2001). Play requires a child to control his/her immediate impulses; however, as Vygotsky asserted, "subjection to rules and the renunciation of impulsive action constitute the path to maximum pleasure in play" (Vygotsky, 1978, p. 99). Vygotsky also remarked that in play, children show greater self-regulation skills than in everyday life. Given that, play represents a zone of proximal development for children to advance their self-regulation skills. Empirical research indicates that playing games (e.g., Red Light Green Light, Simon Says) improves children's inhibition of motor response, working memory, and interference control (Savina et al., 2017; Tominey & McClelland, 2011; Zhao et al., 2015).

Movement

In the past decade, the role of movement in self-regulation has become a focus of extensive research. It was found that children who are more physically active have better motor inhibition (Becker, McClelland, Loprinzi, & Trost, 2014). Motor coordination is also positively associated with inhibition and planning ability (Luz, Rodrigues, & Cordovil, 2015; Rigoli, Piek, Kane, & Oosterlaan, 2012). Further, movement-based interventions improve children's inhibition, working memory, planning, and attention (Chang, Tsai, Chen, & Hung, 2013; Pirrie & Lodewyk, 2012). A study with adults arrived at interesting results: Engaging in proprioceptive activities such as maintaining balance, awareness of different body parts, locomotion, etc., has a positive effect on working memory (Alloway & Alloway, 2015). Physical activity can be beneficial for improving self-regulation in children with ADHD (Pontifex, Saliba, Raine, Picchietti, & Hillman, 2013). Dance and singing activities can also be beneficial for self-regulation skills. It was found that children who are enrolled in music programs demonstrate more mature private speech, an essential self-regulation tool (Winsler, Ducenne, & Koury, 2011). Moreover, engagement in creative dance activities contributes to social competence and better behavioral regulation (Lobo & Winsler, 2006).

Mindfulness

Mindfulness is another self-regulation intervention that has recently received extensive research attention. Mindfulness practice includes activities that require focusing attention on inner experiences (e.g., breathing) and monitoring potential distractions, as well as open and non-judgmental awareness of mental events (Malinowski, 2013). Practicing mindfulness has neurocognitive benefits, as it increases functional connectivity within and between attentional networks (Hasenkamp & Barsalou, 2012). Further, through improving attentional control, mindfulness can exert a positive effect on regulation of emotions and cognitions (Malinowski, 2013). The impact of mindfulness on promoting self-regulation in children has been documented in several studies. Specifically it was found that practicing mindfulness improved attention, emotional control, delayed gratification, prosocial behavior, and executive functioning (Flook, Goldberg, Pinger, & Davidson, 2015; Flook et al., 2010; Schonert-Reichl et al., 2015; Waldemar et al., 2016; Wilson & Dixon, 2010).

Play, Learn, and Enjoy! Curriculum Activities

PLE activities were designed based on the empirical self-regulation research (Flook et al., 2010; Savina et al., 2017; Tominey & McClelland, 2011; Zhao et al., 2015; Semrud-Clikeman et al., 1999; Tamm et al., 2016; Wass et al., 2012) and Vygotskian conceptual principles regarding the development of self-regulation in children (Fernyhough, 2009; Krafft & Berk, 1998; Luria, 1960; Vygotsky, 1978; 1997). More specifically, the following ideas guided the curriculum development:

1. Children develop verbal self-regulation through the internalization of dialogue shared with more skilled partners during a collaborative activity. Following this idea, the PLE curriculum offers many activities that require children to work together, negotiate, and problem solve.

2. Self-regulation develops through the acquisition of cultural tools among which language plays an essential role. Language allows children to plan, reflect upon, and master their own behavior. Many PLE activities require verbal planning, monitoring, and self-evaluation of children's performance.

3. Games with rules and activities that recruit children's imagination are developmentally appropriate contexts to facilitate self-regulation skills in elementary school children. The PLE curriculum is designed as an imaginary journey into a wilderness where children "pretend" that they are rowing a boat, walking in the rainforest, stargazing on the beach, or catching fish. In addition, many activities are designed in a game-like format where children have to follow certain rules.

The PLE curriculum is designed in a thematic format in which children "follow" imaginary characters in their trips to the wilderness. Such a format allows for building one session upon another, which facilitates children's engagement and promotes the continuity of their experiences and accumulation of skills. The curriculum uses social stories to introduce the context and engage children's imaginations. The stories also provide children with an emotional vocabulary and self-regulation scripts, as well as present problem situations to practice problem-solving skills.

The thematic format makes all the activities contextual since they reflect the theme of each session. Activities are sequenced from less to more cognitively demanding, which allows children to master lower-level self-regulation skills before learning more complex skills. The same types of activities are performed in different contexts (e.g., while "traveling" to the oceanside or to a desert) and use different stimuli (e.g., visual searches for berries or for snowflakes). Such instructional strategy promotes flexible use of skills and skill generalization. In addition, children are encouraged to practice skills they learned during the session at home and school. Finally, children complete a self-evaluation at the end of each session, which facilitates self-awareness and an understanding of the skills they master.

Below is a description of PLE activities, which are organized around the self-regulation or socio-emotional skills targeted in each activity. Keep in mind that some activities may engage several skills; for this reason, some activities will be described in more than one section.

Attentional Activities

Find Differences

The *Find Differences* activities train selective visual attention. Children are presented with two pictures of the same object with slight differences and asked to find differences. During this activity, it is important to teach children to use a strategic search (e.g., look for differences section by section, part by part) and to guide their own attention through talking out loud. The content of an activity depends on the theme of the session. For example, children find differences between two pictures of fish (Session 7, Going Fishing) or they search for differences between pictures taken in the desert (Session 13, Going to a Desert—Day 2).

Embedded Pictures

The *Embedded Pictures* activities train selective visual attention, visual tracking, and an ability to ignore interfering visual information. Children are presented with overlaid pictures and asked to identify the target pictures. Examples include identifying rainforest animals in Session 5, Rainforest Trip—Day 2, or desert animals in Session 12, Going to a Desert—Day 1.

Auditory Attention

The *Auditory Attention* activities target selective auditory discrimination and attention skills. In these activities, children have to attend to a target sound embedded in the background sounds. For example, in Session 8, On the Beach, children are asked to identify boat horns as the ocean waves crash in the background. In Session 10, Arctic Excursion—Day 1, children listen for and count the whale sounds amongst bird chatter.

Visual Search

The *Visual Search* activities train selective visual attention and visual interference control. Children are presented with worksheets with target stimuli incorporated in the array of similar stimuli and asked to circle target stimuli while ignoring distractor items. Upon completion, children have to check their work using a key worksheet. The content of the activities depends on the session theme. For example, while on a trip to the rainforest, children are searching for select berries; when on the beach, they are looking for specific seashells; and when in the Arctic, they look for particular snowflakes.

Trail Making

The *Trail Making* activities require selective attention, visual tracking, and interference control skills. Children are given pictures of entangled lines and asked to track lines associated with target items. For example, while on a rainforest trip (Sessions 4 and 5), children "assist" birds in finding their nests, or frogs in hopping on lily pads.

Inhibition Games

Watch for the Signal Games

The *Watch for the Signal* games train response inhibition, working memory, and listening skills. Children are asked a list of questions (e.g., "What is your name?", "Do you like ice cream?", "How many legs do dogs have?") and are required to answer only when a specific signal is given (e.g., placing hands in a prayer sign). Therefore, they have to inhibit their desire to answer when a signal is not given.

Guessing Games

The *Guessing* games require response inhibition, auditory attention, and deductive reasoning. Children are provided with a grid containing pictures of different items depending on the session theme. For example, in Session 1, Getting to Know Each Other, there are pictures of camping items and in Session 9, Going Snorkeling, there are pictures of sea animals. The group leader gives clues about a certain item, and children have to postpone responding until all cues are provided.

Clapping Games

The *Clapping* games train motor interference control and working memory. These games have two trials. During the first trial, children clap when a target word (e.g., "shark") is said and refrain from clapping when other words are said. In the second trial, children have to inhibit an impulse to clap in response to a target word and instead clap in response to other words. The second trial therefore places more demands on inhibition, as children have to withhold a response they have already learned.

Yes and No Games

The *Yes and No* games train response inhibition and working memory. The group leader asks children different questions and requires that children answer them with complete sentences, inhibiting habitual responding with "Yes" or "No." Examples of these questions include "Do you like bananas?", "Do beavers build dams?", and "Do frogs like to sit in chairs?"

Stop Signal Movement Games

The *Stop Signal* games engage motor inhibition, auditory discrimination, and attention skills. Children are asked to move when hearing background sounds, and to stop when they hear a target sound. Examples include Walking with Animals in the Rainforest (Sessions 4 and 5); Catching a Fish (Session 7); Snake Rattling (Sessions 12 and 13); and Walking in the Garden (Session 14).

Memory Activities

Oral Story Recall

Several sessions require children to listen and recall stories. Oral story recall trains children's immediate verbal memory, attention, and expressive and receptive language skills. The children are asked to re-tell a short story related to the session theme. The story might be re-read or read line by line for those with auditory memory, receptive, and expressive language weaknesses.

Working Memory Activities

Many PLE activities involve working memory: i.e., the ability to hold information in an active state in the mind. For example, inhibition games require children to remember the instructions while playing a game. Several movement activities (which will be described later) require working memory, as children have to remember a sequence of actions and execute them when given a signal.

There are also games that specifically target auditory and visual working memory. For example, the *Name a Color* game trains auditory working memory. In this game, one child says a color, and then the next child repeats it and adds his or her color. This process goes around until each person has said a color. Another activity trains visual memory and requires children to remember the animals depicted on a picture.

Collaborative Activities

Collaborative planning and decision-making activities were designed according to the Vygotskian idea about the essential role of social interaction and collaboration for the development of self-regulation. Collaborative activities require a child to coordinate his own perspective, intentions, and goals with those of other children. Furthermore, they require a joint action plan that takes into account the child's own actions and actions of his peers (Tomasello, Carpenter, Call, Behne, & Moll, 2005). Collaborative activities represent a great arena to integrate social and self-regulation skills. Social skills include the ability to identify common goals and intentions, to plan and make decisions collaboratively, take perspectives of others, and negotiate differences. Self-regulation skills include impulse control, working memory, and attention, as collaboration requires an ability to wait for one's turn, inhibit the desire to "push" one's own agenda, and attend to and remember others' opinions. Engagement in collaboration with peers facilitates children's verbal exchanges aimed at generating goals and directing each other's actions. A dialogue with others eventually becomes internalized and transformed into internal self-talk, a verbal self-regulation tool.

Since PLE is designed as series of imaginary trips, planning activities are easily incorporated in the curriculum. For instance, several sessions involve packing a backpack, and children have to work together to identify items they need to take for their trip. The packing a backpack activity imposes limits (e.g., only a certain number of items can be taken), which makes decisions more difficult. Another type of activity used in several sessions requires children to plan among themselves (often using a map) which places they want to visit on a given trip. Several activities require both collaboration and time-management skills. For example, in Session 3, Riverboat Trip—Day 2, children have to "fix" a leak in their boat quickly and calmly.

The role of the group leader during collaborative activities is crucial. The leader should encourage children to ask each other questions, think aloud, plan amongst themselves, and negotiate differences. Throughout the learning process, the adults' assistance should be incrementally withdrawn as children begin to work independently.

Socio-Emotional Activities

Emotion Regulation Activities

Social stories are used to create a venue for practicing emotion-regulation skills. These stories describe emotion-evocative problem situations. Examples of these situations include Fixing the Leak (Session 3), where children are asked to patch a hole in their boat; Crossing the River (Session 5), where children are asked to take turns crossing a precarious place on their trail; and Bumping the Fish (Session 7), where children guide the PLE characters through solving a conflict. Children are asked to generate and practice emotion regulation strategies for anger, anxiety, and fear. Such strategies include identifying an emotion, self-calming, using self-talk, sharing emotions, and asking for help.

Relaxation/Mindfulness Activities

Each session ends with a relaxation/mindfulness activity to teach children stress-reduction techniques and focused attention. Such techniques include muscle relaxation, diaphragmatic breathing, grounding, and guided imagery. All of the activities are contextual, as they reflect the theme of the session. For example, when children take an imaginary trip to the rainforest, they practice guided imagery that involves attending to the sound of rain; when going snorkeling, they practice diaphragmatic breathing; the trip to a desert includes mindful listening to a sound of sand.

Conversational Activities

Conversational games are designed to facilitate active listening, asking questions, taking turns, and maintaining conversation skills. For example, a child shares a statement or two about a given topic; then the next child repeats what the first child said using sentence starters such as, *"As I understand, your favorite animal is…. and you like it because…"* Conversational games also require working memory, as children need to remember what their partner said. In addition, they train impulse control because children have to inhibit their desire to respond prematurely.

In collaborative storytelling activities, children work together on telling a spontaneous story, which trains their active listening, taking turns, planning, short-term memory, and response inhibition skills.

Motor Activities

The PLE motor activities are designed to train children's body awareness, voluntary regulation of movement, visual-motor integration, and emotion regulation. Like other activities, motor activities are contextual. For example, children have to walk across the "obstacle" encountered while traveling across a river or while making their way through a precarious mountain pass. Some activities require gross motor control and balance skills: for example, Crossing the River in Session 5. Other activities involve motor planning and coordination, such as Rowing the Boat in Session 2.

Several motor activities require holding multistep verbal instructions in working memory and executing a sequence of movements. For example, in the Catching a Fish activity (Session 7), children learn several movements and perform them in response to verbal commands. The *Stop Signal* movement games described earlier require coordination of movements with an external signal and train auditory attention and motor inhibition.

Motor activities also allow children to support each other. For example, in some activities, children are encouraged to cheer and motivate one another, but in others they are required to remain calm so that their peers can pay attention and concentrate on the task. Finally, the PLE curriculum consistently uses a unison drumming as a warming-up activity that trains auditory attention, synchronization, and gross motor planning.

References

Alloway, R. G., & Alloway, T. P. (2015). The working memory benefits of proprioceptively demanding training: A pilot study. *Perceptual & Motor Skills: Learning & Memory, 120*(3), 766–775. doi:10.2466/22. PMS.120v18x1

Baddeley, A. D. (2007). *Working memory, thought and action.* Oxford: Oxford University Press.

Barkley, R. A. (1997). *ADHD and the nature of self-control.* New York: Guilford Press.

Barkley, R. A. (1998). Attention deficit hyperactivity disorder (2nd ed.). New York: Guilford Press

Becker, D. R., McClelland, M., Loprinzi, P., & Trost, S. G. (2014). Physical activity, self-regulation, and early academic achievement in preschool children. *Early Education and Development, 25*, 56–70, doi:10.1080/10409289.2013.780505

Berk, L. E., & Potts, M. K. (1991). Development and functional significance of private speech among attention-deficit hyperactivity disordered and normal boys. *Journal of Abnormal Child Psychology, 19*, 357–377.

Berry, D. (2012). Inhibitory control and teacher-child conflict: Reciprocal associations across the elementary-school years. *Journal of Applied Developmental Psychology, 33*, 66–76.

Blair, C. (2002). School readiness: Integrating cognition and emotion in a neurobiological conceptualization of children's functioning at school entry. *American Psychologist, 57*, 111–127.

Bivens, J. A., & Berk, L. E. (1990). A longitudinal study of the development of elementary school children's private speech. *Merrill-Palmer Quarterly, 36*(4), 443–463.

Bull, R., Espy, K. A., & Wiebe, S. A. (2008). Short-term memory, working memory, and executive functioning in preschoolers: Longitudinal predictors of mathematical achievement at age 7 years. *Developmental Neuropsychology, 33*(3), 205–228.

Carlo, G. (2006) Care-based and altruistically based morality. In M. Killen, & J. G. Smetana (Eds.), *Handbook of Moral Development* (551–579). Mahwah, NJ: Lawrence Erlbaum Associates Publishers.

Chang, Y.-K., Tsai, Y.-J., Chen, T.-T., & Hung, T.-M. (2013). The impacts of coordinative exercise on executive function in kindergarten children: An ERP study. *Experimental Brain Research, 225*(2), 187–196. doi: 10.1007/s00221-012-3360-9

Chiu, S., & Alexander, P. A. (2000). The motivational function of preschoolers' private speech. *Discourse Processes, 30*(2), 133–152.

Denham, S. A., Blair, K. A., DeMulder, E., Levitas, J., Sawyer, K., Auerbach-Major, S., & Queenan, P. (2003). Preschool emotional competence: Pathway to social competence? *Child Development, 74*(1), 238–256. doi:10.1111/1467-8624.00533

Eisenberg, N., Fabes, R. A., Guthrie, I. K., & Reiser, M. (2000). Dispositional emotionality and regulation: Their role in predicting quality of social functioning. *Journal of Personality and Social Psychology, 78*(1), 136.

Eisenberg, N., & Spinrad, T. L. (2004). Emotion-related regulation: Sharpening the definition. *Child Development, 75*(2), 334–339. doi:10.1111/j.1467-8624.2004.00674.x

Eisenberg, N., Valiente, C., Spinrad, T. L., Liew, J., Zhou, Q., Losoya, S. H., Reiser, M., & Cumberland, M. (2009). Longitudinal relations of children's effortful control, impulsivity, and negative emotionality to their externalizing, internalizing, and co-occurring behavior problems. *Developmental Psychology, 45*(4), 988–1008. doi:10.1037/a0016213

Fernyhough, C. (2009). Dialogic thinking. In A. Winsler, C. Fernyhough, & I. Montero (Eds.), *Private speech, executive functioning, and the development of verbal self-regulation.* (42–52). New York: Cambridge University Press.

Flook, L., Goldberg, S. B., Pinger, L., & Davidson, R. J. (2015). Promoting prosocial behavior and self-regulatory skills in preschool children through a mindfulness-based kindness curriculum. *Developmental Psychology, 51*(1), 44–51.

Flook, L., Smalley, S. L., Kitil, M. J., Galla, B., Kaiser-Greenland, S., Locke, J., Ishijima, E., & Kasari, C. (2010). Effects of mindful awareness practices on executive functioning in elementary school children. *Journal of Applied School Psychology, 26,* 70–95.

Francis-Smythe, J. A. (2006). Time management. In J. Glicksohn & M. Myslobodsky (Eds.), *Timing the future: The case for a time-based prospective memory.* (143–170) Hackensack, NJ: World Scientific Publishing.

Galyer, K. T., & Evans, I. M. (2001). Pretend play and the development of emotion regulation in preschool children. *Early Child Development and Care, 166*(1), 93–108.

Gauvain, M. (1992). Social influences on the development of planning in advance and during action. *International Journal of Behavioral Development, 15*(3), 377–398. doi: https://doi.org/10.1177/016502549201500306

Goleman, D. (2013). *Focus: The hidden driver of excellence.* New York: HarperCollins.

Graham, A. J., Langberg, J. M., & Epstein, J. N. (2008, August). *Time management intervention for students with ADHD: Pilot data.* Paper presented at 116th annual meeting of the American Psychological Association, Boston, MA.

Graziano, P. A., Reavis, R. D., Keane, S. P., & Calkins, S. D. (2007). The role of emotion regulation in children's early academic success. *Journal of School Psychology, 45*(1), 3–19. doi: 10.1016/j.jsp.2006.09.002

Gross, J. J. (2002). Emotion regulation: Affective, cognitive, and social consequences. *Psychopsysiology, 39*, 281–291.

Gumora, G., & Arsenio, W. F. (2002). Emotionality, emotion regulation, and school performance in middle school children. *Journal of School Psychology, 40*(5), 395–413.

Hasenkamp, W., & Barsalou L. W. (2012). Effects of meditation experience on functional connectivity of distributed brain networks. *Frontiers in Human Neuroscience, 6*(38), 114.

Hofmann, W., Schmeichel, B. J., & Baddeley, A. D. (2012). Executive functions and self-regulation. *Trends in Cognitive Sciences, 16*(3), 174–180.

Hubbard, J. A. (2001). Emotion expression process in children's peer interaction: The role of peer rejection, aggression, and gender. *Child Development, 72*, 1426–1438.

Kopp, C. B. (1982). Antecedents of self-regulation: A developmental perspective. *Developmental Psychology, 18*, 199–214.

Krafft, K. C., & Berk, L. E. (1998). Private speech in two preschools: Significance of open-ended activities and make-believe play for verbal self-regulation. *Early Childhood Research Quarterly, 13*, 637–658.

Lane, K. A. (2012). Visual attention in children: Theories and activities. Thorofare, NJ: SLACK, Inc.

Lengua, L. J. (2003). Associations among emotionality, self-regulation, adjustment problems, and positive adjustment in middle childhood. *Applied Developmental Psychology, 24*, 595–618.

Liew, J. (2012). Effortful control, executive functions, and education: Bringing self- regulatory and social-emotional competencies to the table. *Child Development Perspectives, 6*(2), 105–111.

Linnenbrick, E. A., & Pintrich, P. R. (2000). Multiple pathways to learning and achievement: The role of goal orientation in fostering adaptive motivation, affect, and cognition. In C. Sansone & J. Harackiewicz (Eds.), *Intrinsic and Extrinsic Motivation: The Search for Optimal Motivation and Performance* (195–222). San Diego, CA: Academic Press.

Lobo, Y. B., & Winsler, A. (2006). The effects of a creative dance and movement program on the social competence of Head Start preschoolers. *Social Development, 15*, 501–519.

Luria, A. R. (1960). Experimental analysis of the development of voluntary action in children. In H. P. David & J. C. Brengelmann (Eds.), *Perspectives in personality research* (139–149). New York: Springer.

Luz, C., Rodrigues, L. P., & Cordovil, R. (2015).The relationship between motor coordination and executive functions in 4th grade children. *European Journal of Developmental Psychology, 12*(2), 129–141. doi: 10.1080/17405629.2014.966073

Malinowski, P. (2013). Neural mechanisms of attentional control in mindfulness meditation. *Frontiers in Neuroscience, 7*. doi: 10.3389/fnins.2013.00008

McClelland, M.M., Acock, A.C., & Morrison, F.J. (2006). The impact of kindergarten learning-related skills on academic trajectories at the end of elementary school. *Early Childhood Research Quarterly, 21*(4), 471–490.

McClelland, M. M., Acock, A. C., Piccinin, A., Rhea, S. A., & Stallings, M. C. (2013). Relations between preschool attention span-persistence and age 25 educational outcomes. *Early Childhood Research Quarterly, 28*, 314–324. doi:10.1016/j.ecresq.2012.07.008

Merrell, K. W., & Gimpel, G. A. (1998). Social skills in children and adolescents: Conceptualization, assessment, treatment. Mahwah, NJ: Lawrence Erlbaum Associates.

Miller, D. (2013). Essentials of school neuropsychological assessment. Hoboken, NJ: John Wiley & Sons.

Moffitt, T. E., Arseneault, L., Belsky, D., Dickson, N., Hancox, R. J, Harrington, H., Houts, R., Poulton, R., Roberts, B. W, Ross, S., Sears, M. R., Thomson, W. M., & Caspi, A. (2011). A gradient of childhood self-control predicts health, wealth, and public safety. *Proceedings of the National Academy of Sciences, 108*(7), 2693–2698.

Newton, E., & Jenvey, V. (2011). Play and theory of mind: Associations with social competence in young children. *Early Child Development and Care, 181*(6), 761–773. doi: 10.1080/03004430.2010.486898

Pellegrini, A. D., & Gustafson, K. (2005). Boys' and girls' uses of objects for exploration play and tools in early childhood. In A. D. Pellegrini & P. K. Smith (Eds.), *The nature of play: Great apes and humans* (113–135). New York: Guilford Press.

Piaget, J. (1962). *Play, dreams, and imitation in childhood*. New York: Norton.

Pirrie, A. M., & Lodewyk, K. R. (2012). Investigating links between moderate-to-vigorous physical activity and cognitive performance in elementary school students. *Mental Health and Physical Activity, 5,* 93–98.

Pontifex, M. B., Saliba, B. J., Raine, L. B., Picchietti, D. L., & Hillman, C. H. (2013). Exercise improves behavioral, neurocognitive, and scholastic performance in children with ADHD. *Journal of Pediatrics, 162,* 543–551. doi:10.1016/j.jpeds.2012.08.036

Riggs, N. R., Jahromi, L. B., Razza, R. P., Dillworth-Bart, J. E., & Mueller, U. (2006). Executive function and the promotion of social-emotional competence. *Journal of Applied Developmental Psychology, 27,* 300–309. doi: 10.1016/j.appdev.2006.04.002

Rigoli, D, Piek, J. P., Kane, R., & Oosterlaan, J. (2012). An examination of the relationship between motor coordination and executive functions in adolescents. *Developmental Medicine and Child Neurology, 54*(11), 1025–1031. doi:10.1111/j.1469-8749.2012.04403.x

Röll, J., Koglin, U., & Petermann, F. (2012). Emotion regulation and childhood aggression: Longitudinal associations. *Child Psychiatry and Human Development, 43,* 909–923. doi: 10.1007/s10578-012-0303-4

Saarni, C. (1999). *The development of emotional competence*. New York: The Guilford Press.

Savina, E., Savenkova, I., & Shekotihina, I. (2017, February). *Playing movement games improves self-regulation in children*. Poster presented at the National Association of School Psychologists Annual Convention, San Antonio, TX.

Schaefer, C. E., & Reid, S. E. (2001). *Game play: Therapeutic use of childhood games* (2nd ed.). New York: Wiley.

Schmeichel, B. J., & Demaree, H. A. (2010). Working memory capacity and spontaneous emotion regulation: High capacity predicts self-enhancement in response to negative feedback. *Emotion, 10*(5), 739.

Scholnick, E., & Friedman, S. (1987). *Blueprints for Thinking*. New York: Cambridge University Press.

Schonert-Reichl, K. A., Oberle, E., Lawlor, M. S., Abbott, D., Thompson, K., Oberlander, T. F., & Diamond, A. (2015). Enhancing cognitive and social emotional development through a simple-to-administer mindfulness-based school program for elementary school children: A randomized controlled trial. *Developmental Psychology, 51*(1), 52–66.

Selman, R. L. (2003). Promotion of social awareness: Powerful lessons for the partnership of developmental theory and classroom practice. New York: Russell Sage Foundation.

Semrud-Clikeman, M., Nielsen, K.H., Clinton, A., Leihua, S., Parle, N., & Connor, R.T. (1999). An intervention approach for children with teacher- and parent-identified attention difficulties. *Journal of Learning Disabilities, 32*(6), 581–590.

Swank, J. M. (2008). The use of games: A therapeutic tool with children and families. *International Journal of Play Therapy, 17*(2), 154–167.

Tamm, L., Highs, C., Ames, L., Pickering, J., Silver, C. H., Stavinoha, P., Castillo, C. L., Rintlemann, J., Moore, J., Foxwell, A., Bolanos, S. G., Hines, T., Nakonezny, P. A., & Emslie, G. (2016). Attention training for school-aged children with ADHD: Results of an open trial. *Journal of Attention Disorders, 14*(1), 86–94.

Tomasello, M., Carpenter, M., Call, J., Behne, T., & Moll, H. (2005). Understanding and sharing intentions: The origins of cultural cognition. *Behavioral and Brain Sciences, 28* (5), 675–691.

Tominey, S. L., & McClelland, M. M. (2011). Red light, purple light: Findings from randomized trial using circle time games to improve behavioral self-regulation in preschool. *Early Education & Development, 22*(3), 489–519. doi:10.1080/10409289.2011.574258

Vygotsky, L. S. (1978). The role of play in development. In M. Cole, V. John-Steiner, S. Scribner & E. Souberman (Eds.), *Mind and society: The development of higher mental process* (92–104). Cambridge, MA: Harvard University Press. (Original work published in 1966).

Vygotsky, L. S. (1987). Thinking and speech. In *The collected works of L. S. Vygotsky* (Vol. 1, 37–285). New York: Plenum Press.

Vygotsky, L. S. (1997). The history of development of higher mental functions. In *The collected works of L. S. Vygotsky* (Vol. 4). New York: Plenum Press.

Waldemar, J. O. C, Rigatti, R., Menezes, C. B., Guimaraes, G., Falceto, O., & Heldt, E. (2016). Impact of a combined mindfulness and social-emotional learning program on fifth graders in a Brazilian public school setting. *Psychology and Neuroscience, 9*(1), 79–90.

Wass, S.V., Scerif, G., & Johnson, M. H. (2012). Training attentional control and working memory—Is younger better? *Developmental Review, 32*, 360–387.

Wilson, A. N., & Dixon, M. R. (2010). A mindfulness approach to improving classroom attention. *Journal of Behavioral Health and Medicine, 1,* 137–142.

Winsler, A., Diaz, R. M., & Montero, I. (1997). The role of private speech in the transition from collaborative to independent task performance in young children. *Early Childhood Research Quarterly, 12,* 59–79.

Winsler, A., Ducenne, L., & Koury, A. (2011). Singing one's way to self-regulation: The role of early music and movement curricula and private speech. *Early Education and Development, 22*(2), 274–304. doi:10.1080/10409280903585739

Zentall, S. S, Harper, G. W., & Stormont-Spurgin, M. (1993). Children with hyperactivity and their organizational abilities. *Journal of Educational Research, 87*(2), 112–117.

Zhao, X., Chen, L., Fu, L., & Maes, J. H. R. (2015). "Wesley says": a children's response inhibition playground training game yields preliminary evidence of transfer effects. *Frontiers in Psychology, 6,* 207. http://doi.org/10.3389/fpsyg.2015.00207

Play, Learn, and Enjoy! Curriculum

Getting to Know Each Other

Session Materials

- Chairs placed in a circle
- Camping Items Worksheet 1.1
- Poster-size paper
- Backpack Outline Worksheet 1.2
- Crayons, pencils

Opening Greeting

Leader: "Hello, everyone! I am happy to see you in our group! We are going to do many interesting and fun things. I want to start our meeting with learning about each other. Please tell us your name and share with us your favorite activity. I will start with myself: My name is _____ and I like _____" (*Point to each child in the circle and encourage each to say his/her name and share a favorite activity.*) "Very good! I see that we have several things in common. For example, many of you like to _____ (*name the most frequently chosen activity*)."

Greeting Ritual

Leader: "Now I would like us to make our greeting ritual. How do you want to greet each other every time we meet?" (*Allow children to offer greeting rituals and discuss them with the group with the goal of coming up with an agreement. Help children generate ideas and practice greeting a couple of times.*)

"Every meeting we will do many fun activities together. For each activity, it will be very important to listen to the instructions, follow rules, and pay attention. Let's start practicing those skills right now."

Drumming

Skills: Following directions and motor control

Show the beat by using your hands. For example,——————----(two slow and three fast claps). Ask children to repeat the beat. Then ask the child sitting next to you to show another beat. The group repeats. The next child shows the beat, etc. Keep playing for 3–4 rounds. If children have difficulty generating their own beats, continue demonstrating different beats, but encourage children to help you with ideas.

Meeting Friends

Leader: "It's time to talk about why we're all here together (*make it suspenseful*). We are going to use our imaginations to travel to many different places. For example, we shall take a riverboat ride, we will go to a desert, have fun on a sailboat, go snorkeling, and we shall visit the Arctic. Are you excited about this? Yes, we will have many adventures! We are also going to learn a lot from our journeys! We will use our eyes to see, our ears to listen, and our memory to remember things around us. We will learn how to plan our trips and work together. What are we going to do? (*Solicit responses from children.*)

"Now, let me introduce three friends. Here is Jamal. Jamal likes to be a leader and help others; but, at times, he gets upset when somebody tells *him* what to do. Jamal has a friend and her name is Julia. Julia is a very kind girl, but sometimes she becomes nervous or worried. Jamal and Julia have another good friend, Jose. Jose has a lot of energy! However, at times, he forgets to stop and think before he acts. What did you learn about the three friends? In which ways are they similar to you? In which ways are they different from you? (*Solicit responses from children.*)

"Our friends like doing many things together. One day, not too long ago, Jamal had an idea. 'Let's travel to different places.' Jose immediately replied (*you may want to add dramatic effect*): 'There are so many places I really want to visit. I want to go on a riverboat trip, sail on the ocean, and go snorkeling. I want to do many exciting new things!' 'Whoa, whoa, whoa!,' said Jamal. 'You need to slow down. I like your ideas, but we need to listen to each other and not interrupt.' Julia said, 'Yes, Jose, you are a very good friend, but sometimes you are impatient; you cannot wait. I know a very good game that teaches us to learn to wait. Let's play it!'"

Watch for the Signal

Skills: Attention and inhibition control

Leader: "I am going to ask you different questions. However, you can answer my questions only if I place my hands like this (*make hands like in prayer*)—that will be the signal. If I do not place my hands like that, you cannot answer my question, even if you really want to. So, what do you need to do? (*Solicit responses from children and make sure that they understand the directions correctly.*) All right! Let's start our game. Pay attention to what I say and show." (*Address the following questions to each child in the group and make the hand movement quickly after you ask a question. Alternate the questions with which you pair the hand movement. NOTE: This list can be extended*):

- What's your name?
- Do you like ice cream?
- Can dogs fly?
- What color is your shirt?
- Do you have friends?
- Do cats drink milk?
- Do you like playing games?
- What is your teacher's name?

"Now, we are going to play this game in the opposite way. I am going to ask you different questions. However, when I place my hands like this (*make hands in a prayer*), you cannot answer my questions. Remember, when I place my hands like this (*make hands in a prayer*)—do not to answer this time. So, what do you need to do? (*Solicit responses from children and make sure that they understand the directions correctly.*) All right! Let's start our game." (*Address the following questions to each child in the group and make the hand movement quickly after you ask a question. Alternate the questions with which you pair the hand movement. NOTE: This list can be extended*).

- What's your name?
- Do you like ice cream?
- Can dogs fly?
- What color is your shirt?
- Do you have friends?
- Do cats drink milk?
- Do you like playing games?
- What is your teacher's name?

Discussion about Planning

Leader: "'Good game,' Jose said. 'Can we go on our trips now?' Jamal replied, 'I think we need to plan first.' Jose did not agree. 'Plan? Let's just go! We do not need to spend time planning.' Julia was not sure with whom she agreed.

- What do you think: Should our friends leave right away for their trips, or should they plan their trips before they go?

- Why might it be important to make a plan before going somewhere new?

- What do they need to plan before going on the trip? (*Hint: plan where to go, what to pack, etc.*)

Guessing Game

Skills: Attention and inhibition control

Materials: Camping Items Worksheet 1.1 (one per child)

Leader: "Here are some items that we will need to pack in our backpack for the trip. Let's look at these pictures. (*Prompt children to look carefully at the pictures and verbalize what they see.*) I will read clues about the items, and you will guess which items I am describing. You have to wait until I have read all of the clues.

- "This is something you can put on. (*Pause. If children start shouting out their answers before all the clues are provided, remind them to look carefully at the pictures since several items might fit the description.*) This is something you can put on your feet. (**Boots**)

- This is something that gives directions. (PAUSE). This is something that gives directions and is made of paper. (**Map**)

- This is something that will keep you warm and dry. (PAUSE) This is something that will keep you warm and dry and you can put on. (PAUSE) This is something that will keep you warm and dry, you can put on, and it has laces. (**Boots**)

- This is something that helps you find your way. (PAUSE) This is something that helps you find your way and it has a light. (**Flashlight**)

- This is something you can look through. (PAUSE) This is something you can look through and it takes pictures. (**Camera**)

- This is something you can roll. (PAUSE) This is something you can roll and it gives you directions. (**Map**)"

Packing a Backpack

Skills: Collaboration, perspective taking, inhibition control, active listening

Materials: Backpack outline on poster-size paper; crayons and pencils. (Draw a backpack outline on the paper ahead of time using the Backpack Outline Worksheet 1.2.)

Tell the children that they are going to pack a backpack for their trips. Present a large sheet of paper with an outline of a backpack. Ask the children to think for a minute about an item they each want to put in the backpack. Discuss why the item may be necessary for the trip. Ask the children to take turns and draw items in the outline of the backpack.

Relaxation/Mindfulness

Leader: "On our trip, we might encounter difficult situations. So we need to learn how to calm down; when we are calm, we can solve problems better. Find a comfortable position. We are going to use deep breathing, which can help us feel calm and relaxed. If you notice that you feel worried or stressed, deep breathing can help you feel better.

- Place both hands on your stomach and focus on your breathing, noticing how your stomach moves in and out.
- Breathe in through your nose and out through your mouth.
- Inhale deeply. Fill your lungs slowly.
- Now, breathe out through your mouth.
- Breathe in, breathe out, breathe in, breathe out, breathe in, breathe out, breathe in, and breathe out."

Reflection

Ask children to identify one thing they learned in today's session. Thank everybody for working together and being nice to each other.

Saying Goodbye

Ask children to come up with a "saying goodbye" ritual. After listening to several suggestions, ask the children to choose one. If the children have difficulty creating a ritual, give suggestions and ask them to choose one. The group performs the ritual, and the children are dismissed.

SESSION 2

Riverboat Trip—Day 1

Session Materials

- Chairs placed in the circle
- Backpack Items Worksheet 2.1
- River Map Worksheet 2.2
- Boat Rowing CD Track 1
- Rowboat oars (pre-made oars, butcher or bulletin board paper, rolled and taped to make paper oars)
- Self-Evaluation Worksheet 2.3
- CD player

Greeting Ritual

Leader: "Hello, everyone! Let's start our time together by greeting each other!" After the greeting, say, "Are you ready for our trip? Let's get some energy going!"

Drumming

Skills: Following directions and motor control

Show the beat by using your hands. For example, — - - (one slow and two fast claps). Ask children to repeat the beat. Then ask the child sitting next to you to show another beat. The group repeats. The next child shows the beat, etc. Keep playing for 3–4 rounds. If children have difficulty generating their own beats, continue demonstrating different beats but encourage children to help you with ideas.

Clapping Game: Animals

Skills: Attention and interference control

Leader: "We are going continue our adventure today. But before our trip, let's practice attention and impulse control skills. We will play the 'Clapping' game. You have to listen carefully to what I say. When I say the name of an animal, you will clap. You will not clap if I say something else. So, what do you need to do? (*Solicit responses from children.*) Are you ready? Pay attention!" (*Say one word per second. If children have difficulties, you may say words at a slower pace. Alternatively, if children do not experience difficulty, you may increase speed.*)

LIST: bird, pencil, tomato, fish, cell phone, frog, milk, plum, pizza, chair, truck, onion, computer, squirrel, carrot, bear, fox, table, house.

Play the game for 3–4 rounds.

Leader: "Now we are going to play this game in the opposite way. When I say the name of an animal, you will not clap. You will only clap when I say something other than an animal. So, what do you need to do? (*Solicit responses from children.*) Are you ready?"

LIST: bird, pencil, tomato, fish, cell phone, frog, milk, plum, pizza, chair, truck, onion, computer, squirrel, carrot, bear, fox, table, house.

Play 3–4 rounds.

Oral Story Recall

Skills: Immediate auditory semantic memory

Leader: "Today, we are going to join our new friends Jamal, Julia, and Jose on a riverboat on the Mississippi River. Now, listen very carefully as I tell you information about our riverboat trip and try to remember what I said.

Riverboats have a flat bottom, which is good for traveling in shallow water. They are sometimes called 'water taxis' because they take people across rivers and lakes. Riverboats travel slowly so that their passengers can enjoy nice views along the shore."

Ask children to retell the story. If children have difficulty retelling the story, you may re-read the story. For children with weaknesses in receptive or expressive language, or short-term auditory memory weaknesses, you may read and prompt recall sentence by sentence.

Planning for the Riverboat Trip

Skills: Collaborative planning and decision-making

Materials: River Map Worksheet 2.2

Leader: "Let's help Julia, Jamal, and Jose to plan a riverboat trip."

Show children the map and ask them to look at the map carefully. Ask them to name places on the map. Inform children that they can visit only three places. Give them one minute to think quietly about places each of them wants to visit. Instruct them not to shout out their answers. Ask each child which places he or she wants to visit and write down answers. Engage children in negotiation if they want to visit different places. Teach them to take in the perspectives of others and compromise.

Ask the children to develop rules they want to follow on their trip. Make sure that children have rules for safety and for positive interpersonal relationships. Discuss whether the children collaborated well and what they want to do in the future to improve their collaboration.

Packing a Backpack

Materials: Backpack Items Worksheet 2.1 (one per group)

Skills: Collaborative planning and decision-making

Leader: "Now, we need to pack our backpacks. Do you remember what we decided to do on our trip? (*Solicit responses from children.*) Look carefully at these items and think about things that you want to take on this trip. We can take ONLY three things because we do not want our boat to be too heavy. Keep in mind what we planned to do on this trip. (*Give children 30 seconds to think.*) Now, tell the group what you want to take and why." (*Write down children's answers. Make sure that children take into account their plan: for example, they need a fishing pole if they want to go fishing, or they do not need to take a lot of water because they can get it at the marina store. Summarize what children generated and finalize the list.*)

Rowing the Boat

Skills: Motor control and gross-motor planning

Materials: Boat Rowing CD Track 1; butcher or bulletin board paper; scotch or masking tape; CD player

Provide one "oar" per two children (about 2.5 feet long). To make the oars, use butcher block, bulletin board, or poster paper. Roll tightly and tape around the circumference of the rolled paper in at least three places in order to make an oar-like shape.

Ask children to line up the chairs in pairs (beside one another); organize pairs to face the back of the pair in front of them. Have each pair hold one oar; the oar should be placed in front of children at the length of their extended arms. Make sure that children have enough space in front of them. Children must row with their oars simultaneously.

Leader: "We are going to practice rowing with our oars so that our boat moves slowly through the water. We are going to work together. Go ahead and row slowly." (*Give children 15 seconds to row slowly and ensure that they are rowing at the same speed as one another.*) "Great. Now, let's practice rowing with our oars quickly. Go ahead and row faster, but be careful because we have to stay all together." (*Give children 10 seconds to row quickly and ensure that they are rowing at the same speed as one another.*)

"Now, we are boarding! Watch your step as you board the riverboat. The river has slow water, but watch out because the water can change suddenly and become very fast up ahead! When the water goes fast, I want you to paddle quickly. When the water goes slow, I want you to paddle slowly."

Play the Boat Rowing CD Track 1. When the track begins, instruct the children to paddle with their oars to follow the recording speed.

As the children paddle, give comments like "Oh no, we've reached a rough part of the water. Paddle fast to keep going forward!" or "We have made it back to the still waters. Paddle slowly!"

Arriving at the Shore

Leader: "Finally, we have arrived at the shore. We used our muscles to paddle through the water, and when the water became rough, we paddled even harder! When we use our muscles, they tighten up so we need to loosen them. We can do it by stretching." Show children simple stretching and ask them to repeat after you.

Relaxation/Mindfulness

Leader: "Now, let's practice deep breathing again as we did last time. Remember, it can help us feel calm and relaxed.

- Place one hand on your stomach and feel it move in and out with each breath.
- Place both hands on your stomach and focus on your breathing, noticing how your stomach moves in and out.
- Breathe in through your nose and out through your mouth.
- Inhale deeply. Fill your lungs slowly.
- Now, breathe out through your mouth.
- Breathe in, breathe out, breathe in, breathe out, breathe in, breathe out, breathe in, breathe out."

Reflection

Materials: Self-Evaluation Worksheet 2.3 (one per child). These worksheets will be used for all sessions.

Make children familiar with the skills presented in the self-evaluation worksheet. Discuss how they performed on those skills **as a group**. Thank everybody for working together and being nice to each other. Ask children to practice skills learned in today's session at home and school.

Saying Goodbye

The group performs the goodbye ritual and the children are dismissed.

Riverboat Trip — Day 2

Session Materials

- Chairs placed in the circle
- Looking for Animals Worksheets 3.1, 3.2, and 3.3
- Bird Trail Making Worksheet 3.4 and Bird Trail Making—Key Worksheet 3.5
- Worksheet templates for a Boat Hole 3.6 and Puzzle Pieces 3.7
- Self-Evaluation Worksheet 2.3
- Boat Rowing CD Track 1 and Forest Sounds CD Track 2
- CD player
- Pencils

Greeting Ritual

Leader: "Hello, everyone! Let's start our time together by greeting each other!" Ask children to share which skills they practiced since the last meeting.

Drumming

Skills: Attention and following directions

Leader: "Are you ready for our trip today? Let's get some energy going!"

This time, show the beat using hands and thighs. For example, tap with your left hand twice on your left thigh and three times with your right hand on your right thigh. Then ask the child sitting next to you to show another beat. The group repeats. The next child shows the beat, etc. Keep playing for 3–4 rounds.

Conversational Activity

Skills: Conversation and working memory

Leader: "Now, we are going to practice our attention and listening skills. We are going to share our favorite animal. Tell us what your favorite animal is and why you like it. You have to listen to each other carefully because we will have to repeat what you just heard from your partner."

Ask a child who sits on your left to start sharing and then repeat what he/she said by saying, "As I understood, your favorite animal is… And you like it because…" After modeling, continue the activity.

Clapping Game: Animals

Skills: Attention and interference control

Leader: "We are going to play the 'Clapping' game to practice attention and impulse control skills. You have to listen carefully to what I say. When I say the name of an animal, you will clap. You will not clap if I say something else. You have to use your attention skills. Are you ready?" (*Say one word per second. If children have difficulties, you may say words at the slower pace. Alternatively, if children do not experience difficulty, you may increase speed.*)

LIST: bird, pencil, tomato, fish, cell phone, frog, milk, plum, pizza, chair, truck, onion, computer, squirrel, carrot, bear, fox, table, house.

Play the game for 3–4 rounds.

Leader: "Now we are going to play this game in the opposite way. When I say the name of an animal, you will not clap. You will only clap when I say something other than an animal. Are you ready?"

LIST: bird, pencil, tomato, fish, cell phone, frog, milk, plum, pizza, chair, truck, onion, computer, squirrel, carrot, bear, fox, table, house.

Play 3–4 rounds.

Looking for Animals

Skills: Visual short-term memory

Materials: Looking for Animals Worksheets 3.1, 3.2, and 3.3.

Leader: "Today, we are going to continue to travel down the Mississippi River with our friends. Let's check in with our friends, Jamal, Julia, and Jose to see what they've been up to. While paddling their boat, our friends noticed many interesting things around them. Let's take a look at what they saw."

Present Looking for Animals Worksheet 3.1 (one per group). Ask children to look carefully and memorize items on the picture. Turn the paper over and ask the children:

- Which animals did you see?
- How many fish were in the water?
- How many trees were in the picture?
- Which animals were near the trees?

If children have difficulty, you may expose them again to the picture.

Present Looking for Animals Worksheet 3.2 (one per group). Ask children to look carefully and memorize items on the picture. Turn the paper over and ask the children:

- Which animals did you see?
- Which animals were in the water?
- How many fish were in the water?
- How many trees were in the picture?
- What animal was near the tree?
- What else was in the picture?

If children have difficulty, you may expose them again to the picture.

Present Looking for Animals Worksheet 3.3 (one per group). Ask children to look carefully and memorize items on the picture. Turn the paper over and ask the children:

- Which animals were in the picture?
- How many fish were in the water?
- Which animals were near the trees?
- How many frogs did you notice?

If children have difficulty, you may expose them again to the picture.

Bird Trail Making

Skills: Visual attention and tracking

Materials: Bird Trail Making Worksheet 3.4 and Bird Trail Making—Key Worksheet 3.5 (one per child)

Leader: "Oh, there are birds trying to get to their nests. See if you can help the birds using your attention skills. Take a moment to see which winding flight path each bird should take." Have children trace the paths to each correct nest with a pencil. Use the Key worksheet to check correct paths.

Rowing the Boat

Skills: Motor control and planning

Materials: Boat Rowing CD Track 1; CD player; one "oar" per two children.

Seating Arrangement

This time, have two groups of pairs facing one another. Have each pair hold one oar; the oar should be placed in front of the children at the length of their extended arms. One group will row the oar clockwise and the other group that is facing will row counterclockwise.

    Leader: "Now we are going to row out boats as we did last time. We are going to work together. Go ahead and row slowly." (*Give children 15 seconds to row slowly and ensure that they are rowing at the same speed as one another.*) "Great. Now, let's practice rowing with our oars quickly. Go ahead and row faster, but be careful because we have to stay all together." (*Give children 10 seconds to row quickly and ensure that they are rowing at the same speed as one another.*)

    "When the water goes fast, I want you to paddle quickly. When the water goes slowly, I want you to paddle slowly."

    Play the Boat Rowing CD Track 1 on the CD. When the track begins, instruct the children to paddle with their oars to follow the recording speed.

    As the children paddle, give comments like "Oh no, we've reached a rough part of the water. Paddle fast to keep going forward!" or "We have made it back to the still waters. Paddle slowly!"

Fixing the Leak

Skills: Emotion regulation

Leader: "Listen, what will happen next to our friends? Suddenly, the boat hit a big rock and has started to leak! A leak in the boat means that the boat might sink! When they discovered the leak in the boat, Julia and Jose became very nervous and worried. Their hands started shaking, and their hearts beat very fast! (*Imitate worry with your body language.*) Worry is a feeling many people would have in such a stressful situation. Jamal said, 'I know that you are worried, but we need to solve the problem. We need to calm down so that we can fix the boat!' What could our friends do to calm down?" Ask children to generate strategies. Strategies may include taking deep breaths, counting to ten, talking about feelings, etc. Discuss the pros and cons of each strategy.

Role Play

Ask volunteers to play Julia, Jose, and Jamal and tell the children their lines.

Julia: "Oh no! There is a leak! What do we do? What do we do?"

Jose: "I'm scared! Maybe we should swim to shore!"

Jamal: "I know that you are worried, but we need to solve the problem. We need to calm down so that we can fix the boat! Let's see, how could we solve the problem?"

Ask children to use emotion regulation strategies to calm down.

Fixing the Leak (Continued)

Skills: Collaborative problem solving

Materials: Templates for a Boat Hole 3.6 and Puzzle Pieces 3.7. The "puzzle pieces" need to be cut out beforehand. Lamination will allow for repeated use.

Leader: "Great job. It was important for the friends to calm down because they had to fix the leak. Let's help them to solve their problem." Use the template for a hole and the matching template with puzzle pieces.

"Let's look at pieces we have to plug the hole. Remember we need to fix it very quickly! Work together and help each other." Show children the Boat Hole template and give them puzzle pieces. Ask children to collaborate quickly, but as calmly as possible to decide how to place the puzzle pieces in order to plug the hole.

"Very good. Think about how important it was for our two friends to calm down. When they were calm, they were able to solve the problem! That is true for us, too. Remember that feeling worried is okay, but once we understand how we feel, we can take use strategies to calm ourselves down. Then we can find a solution to the problem!"

Relaxation/Mindfulness

Materials: Forest Sounds CD Track 2 (5 minutes); CD player.

Leader: "Now let's practice relaxation skills, which can also help us with worries. Find a comfortable position. (*Give specific directions, depending on your constraints with space. Use a gentle and quiet voice.*) Close your eyes. We are going to use our imaginations now. Remember, this is a quiet activity, so only I will be talking. You will be using your ears to listen. Take a deep breath…Breathe in…. and out…in…and out…We are going on our pretend journey to the woods…(*Play the Forest Sounds CD Track 2.*) We are walking together through the woods on a gravel trail. Breathe in…. and out…in…and out…It is a beautiful, sunny day. We feel the warmth of the sun on our faces…Breathe in…. and out…in…and out…We see the small pebbles and rocks on the trail. When we step on the soil, it feels soft under our boots. When we step on pebbles, we feel bumps underneath our feet…Breathe in…. and out…in…and out…As we continue walking down the path, we notice how green the trees are. We see yellow flowers…and an orange and black butterfly resting on one of them. Its wings slowly open and close, as it takes a rest, too…Breathe in…. and out…in…and out…We now begin to notice the sounds in the woods. We hear soft sounds of leaves in the trees…We hear the sounds of birds chirping…We hear the pebbles under our feet…It is quiet except for these sounds…Breathe in…. and out…in…and out…Slowly, we begin to make our way up a hill. We are leaving the woods now. When you are ready, open your eyes."

Reflection

Materials: Self-Evaluation Worksheet 2.3 (one per child)

Ask children to identify one thing they learned in today's session. Guide the discussion based on the skills listed in the self-evaluation worksheet from Session 2 (which will be used for all sessions). This time, after the discussion, have **each child** complete a self-evaluation on each skill reviewed. With immature children, review each skill together. Thank everybody for working together and being nice to each other. Ask children to practice skills learned in today's session at home and school. You may want to provide each child with a folder or binder to keep their self-evaluation worksheets to track their progress.

Saying Goodbye

The group performs the ritual and the children are dismissed.

Rainforest Trip—Day 1

Session Materials

- Chairs placed in a circle
- A backpack; various items including boxes, shoes, water bottles, and other items that can fit into a backpack
- Berries #1 Worksheets 4.1 and Berries #1—Key Worksheets 4.2
- Frog Trail Making Worksheet 4.3 and Frog Trail Making—Key Worksheet 4.4
- Rainforest Animals CD Track 3 and Soft Rain Track 4
- Self-Evaluation Worksheet 2.3
- Pencils
- CD player

Greeting Ritual

Leader: "Hello, everyone! Let's start our time together by greeting each other!" Ask the children to share if they practiced the skills learned in the previous session.

Yes and No Game

Skills: Attention and interference control

Leader: "Before we set off on our next adventure, let's practice another skill that we will be using today. We are going to play a 'Yes and No' game to train our attention and impulse control skills. I am going to ask you different questions. However, you can answer my questions **only** with a complete sentence. You cannot answer with 'Yes' or 'No.' For example, if I ask you, 'Do you like ice cream?' you cannot say 'Yes' or 'No.' Instead, you have to say, 'I like ice cream' or 'I do not like ice cream.'" Proceed with the game, directing questions at each child. (NOTE: *The list of questions can be extended.*)

- Do you like bananas?
- Can birds fly?
- Can fish walk?
- Do you have a dog?
- Is grass blue?
- Do you like apples?
- Can deer fly?
- Do cars drive in the river?
- Do frogs sit in chairs?
- Is grass green?
- Do you have a cat?

Oral Story Recall

Skills: Immediate verbal memory, receptive and expressive language

Leader: "Today, Jamal, Julia, and Jose are going to visit the rainforest in Brazil, and we are going along, too! I will tell you a story about the rainforest. You will listen carefully and remember what I have said because it will be important for planning our trip.

A rainforest is a very warm and wet place, with many plants, animals, and insects. It can be dark inside because the tall trees have so many leaves that they make a tent above our heads. So, very little sunlight enters the rainforest. But don't worry! Not all of the rainforest is dark. That is good because we can see many plants and animals."

Ask the children, "What did you learn about rainforests?" Help them if they have difficulty remembering details. You may re-read the story.

Packing a Backpack

Materials: A backpack; various items including boxes, shoes, water bottles, etc.

Skills: Time management and collaboration

Leader: "Now we are going to pack our backpacks. You have to work fast but carefully. Make sure that you help each other." Place items in different places in the room away from the backpack. Select one child to be in charge of packing the backpack. The other children will bring items to the packer.

Remind children that they need to work together. Give children one minute for packing. At the end, discuss how they did, what went well, and what could have been done to be more efficient and cooperative. Switch to allow others to be in charge of packing.

Looking for Berries

Materials: Berries #1 Worksheet 4.1 and Berries #1—Key Worksheet 4.2 (one per child); pencils

Skills: Interference control

Leader: "When our friends arrived at the rainforest, they saw many beautiful berries. They wanted to pick and eat them. However, Jamal said, 'Do not touch those berries! Some of them may be poisonous!' Julia asked if Jamal knew which berries were edible. He showed some edible berries. Now, we are going to pick berries with our friends."

Give children the Berries #1 Worksheet 4.1 with one target berry and explain that only the target berry is edible. Ask the children to look carefully at the target berry and say, "Some berries may look alike, but they have slight differences." Ask children to circle ONLY the "edible berry" on the worksheet and do it as fast as they can without making mistakes. Note that the second page has a different target berry. After they finish, ask them to check their sheets for errors using the worksheets Berries #1—Key Worksheet 4.2.

Walking with Animals in the Rainforest

Materials: Rainforest Animals CD Track 3; CD player

Skills: Motor inhibition

Leader: "Now we are ready to explore the deepest parts of the rainforest and discover the types of animals that might live here. Many animals are very friendly and make beautiful sounds, like the call of birds. However, other animals can be dangerous and we do not want to get close to them. We should be especially careful if we hear any animals growling. When you hear birds singing, you can walk, but when you hear a growling sound, you have to freeze. Are you ready?"

(*Play the Rainforest Animals CD Track 3 on the CD.*) The children walk, but then freeze when they hear growling. When the growling stops, they may continue walking.

Frog Trail Making

Materials: Frog Trail Making Worksheet 4.3 (one per child); pencils

Skills: Visual attention and tracking

Leader: "Let's keep an eye out for animals we may see. Oh, look! There are frogs trying to get to land by hopping across lily pads. Let's find out how many stops each frog will make on the lily pads. Take a moment to see which winding path each frog should take." Have the children trace the paths to the correct lily pad with a pencil. Use the Frog Trail Making—Key Worksheet 4.4 to check correct paths.

Relaxation/Mindfulness

Materials: Soft Rain CD Track 4 (5 minutes); CD player

Leader: "Now we have come to a quiet place in the rainforest. Find a comfortable position. (*Give specific directions, depending on your constraints with space. Use a gentle and quiet voice.*) Close your eyes. We are going to use our imaginations now. Remember, this is a quiet activity, so only I will be talking. You will be using your ears to listen. Take a deep breath. Breathe in...and out...in...and out...We are going to pretend that we are in the rainforest. A dark cloud brought a light rain. (*Play the Soft Rain CD Track 4 on the CD.*) Imagine the sound of the rain as each drop lands on the leaves of the forest. Breathe in...and out...in...and out...It is a gentle rain...Listen to the rain. Breathe in...and out...in...and out...Now imagine the tickly feeling of the rain on your body as it gently touches your skin. Breathe in...and out...in...and out...Feel the rain. Feel your stomach rise and fall as you slowly breathe in and out. Breathe in...and out...in...and out...Feel the tiny beads of cool rainwater. Breathe in...and out...in...and out...Breathe in...and out...in...and out...Now, take one more deep breath and open your eyes. Feel the sunshine on your face as you stretch your body."

Reflection

Materials: Self-Evaluation Worksheet 2.3 (one per child)

Ask the children to identify one thing they learned in today's session. Guide the discussion based on the skills listed in the self-evaluation worksheet. After the discussion, have each child complete the self-evaluation on each skill reviewed. With immature children, review each skill together. Thank everybody for working together and being nice to each other. Ask the children to practice the skills learned in today's session at home and school.

Saying Goodbye

The group performs the ritual and the children are dismissed.

Rainforest Trip — Day 2

Session Materials

- Chairs placed in a circle
- Amazon Animals Worksheet 5.1
- Berries # 2 Worksheets 5.2 and Berries # 2—Key Worksheets 5.3
- Rainforest Animals CD Track 3 and Soft Rain CD Track 4
- Masking tape
- Self-Evaluation Worksheet 2.3
- 10–13 small objects: e.g., poker chips or paper clips
- Pencils
- CD player

Greeting Ritual

Leader: "Hello, everyone! Let's start our time together by greeting each other!" Ask children to share which skills they practiced since the last meeting.

Drumming

Skills: Attention and following directions

Leader: "Are you ready for our trip today? Let's get some energy going!" Show the beat, for example, using hands and feet. Have children repeat the beat. Ask a child sitting next to you to make another beat and have the group repeat it. The next child shows the beat, etc. Keep playing for 3–4 rounds.

Name a Color

Skills: Working memory

Leader: "Today, we are going to continue our journey through the rainforest. Let's practice our memory skills before we go on our journey." Have one child in the group say a color. Then the next person says the color that was said before her and adds her color. Go around until each person has said a color.

Clapping Game: Colors

Skills: Attention and interference control

Leader: "We are going to play the 'Clapping Game.' You have to listen carefully to what I say. When I say the name of a color, you will clap. You will not clap if I say something else. Are you ready?"

   LIST: parrot, blue, flower, red, monkey, orange, rain, trees, yellow, orange, moss, canopy, spider, blue, ant, jaguar, leaves, green, caterpillar, red, blue.

   Play the game 3–4 rounds.

   Leader: "Now we are going to play this game in the opposite way. When I say the name of a color, you will not clap. You will only clap when I say something other than a color. Are you ready?"

   LIST: parrot, blue, flower, red, monkey, orange, rain, trees, yellow, orange, moss, canopy, spider, blue, ant, jaguar, leaves, green, caterpillar, red, blue.

Play the game 3–4 rounds.

Taking Pictures

Skills: Selective attention

Materials: Amazon Animals Worksheet 5.1 (one per child)

Leader: "Our friends took pictures of the animals during their trip to Amazon rainforest. However, the pictures got mixed up. Let's help Julia, Jose, and Jamal to sort them out."

   Present children with the worksheet and direct their attention to the target items on the top. Ask children to identify which target animals are presented in the overlaid pictures. Note that the overlaid pictures also contain other animals that are not present in the target group.

Crossing the River

Skills: Emotion regulation

Materials: Masking tape

Lay masking tape on the floor to represent a log.

Leader: "Our friends continued walking through the rainforest. Suddenly, they came to a place where the river crossed their path! The only way they could continue through the rainforest was to cross this river to get to the other side. They found a log and placed the log from one side over the river to the other, so that it made a bridge. Our friends were happy that they solved their problem. They were getting ready to cross, but suddenly Julia became very anxious; she said, 'I cannot cross the river by walking on that log. What if I fall in?!' She started breathing very fast. Jamal noticed Julia's worry and said, 'Do not worry, Julia! The river is not deep or fast, and I will help you to cross!' Julia shook her head, 'No' and sat down on the trail. She was too worried to try. Let's help Julia feel more calm and relaxed. We can do this by helping her to slow her breathing. We'll all try it together to support Julia."

"Let's put one hand on our stomachs, so that we can check our breathing. First, we will take a deep breath through our noses like you are smelling the rainforest flowers. Now, breathe out slowly like you are blowing the rain clouds away." Continue, saying, "Smell the rainforest flowers. Blow the rain clouds away." Repeat five times.

Crossing the River (Continued)

Skills: Motor control

"After we practiced breathing, Julia calmed down. Now, we have to think about how we are going to cross the river. When walking across, we need to remember three things: First, we have to walk in a straight line with one foot completely in front of the other. (*Show to the children.*) Second, we have to hold our arms straight out for balance. Birds and airplanes do this so that they don't fall down to one side. (*Show to the children.*) Third, we need to take deep breaths while we are walking so we will not get anxious."

Children gather into a group, as if on one side of the "river." Children walk across the "log" one at a time. Encourage children to cheer and motivate one another.

Looking for Berries

Skills: Selective attention

Materials: Berries # 2 Worksheet 5.2 and Berries # 2—Key Worksheet 5.3 (one per child); pencils

Leader: "Our friends decided to pick more berries. This time two berries will be edible and the others will not." Give children a Berries # 2 Worksheet

5.2 with two target berries and explain that these two berries are edible. Ask children to circle ONLY "edible berries" on the worksheet and do it as fast as they can without making mistakes. Note that the second page has different target berries. After the children finish, ask them to check their sheets for errors using the Berries # 2—Key Worksheet 5.3.

Walking with Animals in the Rainforest

Skills: Motor inhibition

Materials: Rainforest Animals CD Track 3; 10–13 small objects: e.g., poker chips or paper clips.

Spread paper clips or poker chips around the room. These will be "berries."

Leader: "Now, we are all going to walk through the forest to pick berries! We will pretend the (paperclips or poker chips) are berries. Just remember, when you hear birds singing, you can walk, but when you hear a growling sound, you have to freeze. Are you ready?" Play the Rainforest Animals CD Track 3 on the CD. The children will walk and pick up berries, but then freeze when they hear a growling sound.

Relaxation/Mindfulness

Materials: Soft Rain CD Track 4 (5 minutes); CD player

Leader: "Now we have come to a quiet place in the rainforest. Find a comfortable position. (*Give specific directions, depending on your constraints with space. Use a gentle and quiet voice.*) Close your eyes. We are going to use our imaginations now. Remember, this is a quiet activity, so only I will be talking. You will be using your ears to listen. Take a deep breath…Breathe in…. and out…in…and out…We are going to pretend that we are in the rainforest…(*Play the Soft Rain CD Track 4.*) The dark cloud brought a light rain. Imagine the sound of the rain as each drop lands on the leaves of the forest….Breathe in…and out…in…and out…It is a gentle rain…Hear the rain…Breathe in…and out…in…and out…Now imagine the tickly feeling of the rain on your body as it gently touches your skin…Breathe in…and out…in…and out…Feel the rain…Feel your stomach rise and fall as you slowly breathe in and out…Breathe in…and out…in…and out…Feel the tiny beads of cool rainwater…Breathe in…and out…in…and out…Breathe in…and out…in…and out…Now, take one more deep breath and open your eyes. Feel the sunshine on your face as you stretch your body."

Reflection

Materials: Self-Evaluation Worksheet 2.3 (one per child)

Ask children to identify one thing they learned in today's session. Guide the discussion based on the skills listed in the self-evaluation worksheet. After the discussion, have each child complete self-evaluation on each skill reviewed. With immature children, review each skill together. Thank everybody for working together and being nice to each other. Ask children to practice skills learned in today's session at home and school.

Saying Goodbye

The group performs the ritual and the children are dismissed.

SESSION 6

Going Sailing

Session Materials

- Chairs placed in a circle
- Weather Forecast Worksheet 6.1
- Islands Map Worksheet 6.2
- Trading Post Items Worksheet 6.3
- Sailing CD Track 5 and Stargazing CD Track 6
- Self-Evaluation Worksheet 2.3
- CD Player

Greeting Ritual

Leader: "Hello, everyone! Let's start our time together by greeting each other!" Ask children to share which skills they practiced since the last meeting.

Clapping Game: Shark

Skills: Attention and interference control

Leader: "Today, we have an exciting trip to the ocean. But before we will go, we need to practice attention and impulse control skills. We will play the 'Clapping' game again. You have to listen carefully to what I say. When I say the word 'shark,' you will clap. You will not clap if I say something else. So, what do you need to do? (*Solicit responses from children.*) Are you ready?" (*Say one word per second. If children have difficulties, you may say words at the slower pace. Alternatively, if children do not experience difficulty, you may increase speed.*)

    LIST: shark, boat, wave, fish, seaweed, shark, sail, fishing pole, shark, life jacket, pail, sand, crab, shell, shark, shark, rock, turtle, sun, shark, umbrella, compass, shark.

Play the game for 3–4 rounds.

Leader: "Now we are going to play this game in the opposite way. You cannot clap when I say 'shark.' You will clap when I say something else. Are you ready?"

LIST: shark, boat, wave, fish, seaweed, shark, sail, fishing pole, shark, life jacket, pail, sand, crab, shell, shark, shark, rock, turtle, sun, shark, umbrella, compass, shark.

Play 3–4 rounds.

Oral Story Recall

Leader: "One day, our friends decided to go on a sailing trip. Jose got very excited; he wanted to go immediately. However, he remembered it is good to plan what you want to do, so you will be prepared. He said to his friends, 'Let's plan our trip.' They decided that they want to spend time on the beach, go fishing, and go snorkeling. Now, listen carefully and remember what they have discussed.

It is best to go to the beach when it is sunny but not very hot so the sand does not burn our feet. Fishing is best when it is cloudy because you do not want to be burned by the sun. For snorkeling, you need a lot of sun in order to see the fish and other sea life."

Ask children to repeat what the friends decided to do. Help children if they had difficulty recalling the details of the story.

Planning a Trip

Skills: Collaborative planning

Materials: Weather Forecast Worksheet 6.1 (one per group); Islands Map Worksheet 6.2 (one per group)

Leader: "Now, let's all take a close look at the map. (*Present children with the Islands Map Worksheet 6.2.*)

On this map, you will see three islands. There is a Coral Reef Island, and here we want to snorkel. We will go to the Fishing Island to catch fish. Last, there is a Beach Island with beautiful sand and blue water. What did you learn about the islands? (*Solicit responses from children.*)

Now, look carefully at the weather forecast for the next three days. (*Present the weather forecast.*) It looks like the weather will be cloudy on the first day; it will be sunny but not hot on the second day; and it will be sunny and hot on the third day. Which islands should we go to on their first day? On their second? On their third?"

Guide children in planning the three-day trip taking into consideration the weather forecast.

"After considering all of the activities and the weather for the next three days, our friends decided to go fishing on the first day, to the beach on the second day, and snorkeling on the third day."

Visiting the Trading Post

Skills: Collaborative decision-making

Materials: Trading Post Items Worksheet 6.3 (one per group)

Leader: "Our friends first decided to shop at the Trading Post to buy things that will be necessary for the first day of the trip. Now think about things that you want to take on this trip. We can take ONLY five things because we do not want our sailboat to be too heavy. Keep in mind what we planned to do on this trip." Give children one minute to think.

"Now, tell the group what you want to take and why." Write down the children's answers. Make sure that the children take into account their plan: for example, they need a fishing pole and a snorkel. It is important that children understand that they can share things (e.g., fishing pole). Summarize what the children generated and finalize the list.

Sailing

Skills: Auditory working memory, selective attention, and motor control

Materials: Sailing CD Track 5, CD player

Leader: "The friends are starting their sailing adventure and so are we! Sailboats are propelled by the wind. There are large sails that have to be moved so that they can catch the wind. There is a lot to learn on a sailboat, like new words and special commands.

Let's learn some new commands. When the captain says, 'Tack starboard,' you will need to grab the sails and lean to the right side of the boat like this (*demonstrate bending at the waist and pantomiming grabbing sail line*). When the captain says, 'Tack port,' you will need to grab the sail and bend your body the left side of the boat like this (*demonstrate bending at the waist and pantomiming grabbing sail line*). When the captain says, 'Ready about,' you should stand at attention like this..." (*model to children how to stand up straight with hands by their sides facing forward*). Practice for 2–3 rounds before playing the Sailing CD Track 5.

"The winds have picked up, and the captain needs your help sailing the boat through the rough waters! You will need to follow the captain's commands quickly. Listen carefully so that you know what to do. When the captain says a command, do it quickly!"

Collaborative Storytelling

Skills: Listening and inhibition control

Leader: "What a wonderful sailing adventure! After sailing the high seas, our friends decided that it was time to head back to shore. Once there, Julia, Jamal, and Jose sat at a bonfire. It was a beautiful evening! They could see many stars in the night sky. Julia said to her friends, 'Let's tell stories! I can start. Once upon a time, there were three friends who liked to travel together. One day…' How can we add to that story? Let's each take a turn." Point to the child sitting next to you in the circle and ask him or her to continue the story. The story goes around the circle.

Relaxation/Mindfulness

Materials: Stargazing CD Track 6 (5 minutes); CD player

Leader: "Now that our friends are finished telling stories, they have decided to do a mindfulness activity and we are going to do it too. Make yourself comfortable, sitting on the deck of the ship. (*Give specific directions, depending on your constraints with space. Use a gentle and quiet voice.*) Close your eyes. We are going to use our imaginations now. Remember, this is a quiet activity, so only I will be talking. You will be using your ears to listen. Take a deep breath…Breathe in…. and out…in…and out… (*Play the Stargazing CD Track 6.*) The water is calm and the ship is still. You can hear the water softly lap on the shore. Breathe in…. and out…in…and out… As you look up at the dark sky, you see the first stars appear…. then another…and then another…. and another…Breathe in…. and out…in…and out… The stars twinkle and glow and you see more and more appear. Breathe in…. and out…in…and out… Notice how some stars shine brightly, while others give off a dim light. You can no longer count the stars, as the clear night sky is filled with them. Breathe in…. and out…in…and out…in…. and out…in…and out… You feel relaxed and enjoy the still night. Breathe in…. and out…in…and out… Now take a deep breath, open your eyes, and stretch. Notice the sense of relaxation that stays with you."

Reflection

Materials: Self-Evaluation Worksheet 2.3 (one per child)

Ask children to identify one thing they learned in today's session. Guide the discussion based on the skills listed in the self-evaluation worksheet. After the discussion, have each child complete self-evaluation on each skill reviewed. With immature children, review each skill together. Thank everybody for working together and being nice to each other. Ask children to practice skills learned in today's session at home and school.

Saying Goodbye

The group performs the ritual and the children are dismissed.

Going Fishing

Session Materials

- Chairs placed in a circle
- Fishing Poles Worksheet 7.1 and Fishing Poles—Key Worksheet 7.2
- Find Five Differences Worksheet 7.3 and Find Five Differences—Key Worksheet 7.4
- Soft Waves CD Track 7
- Self-Evaluation Worksheet 2.3
- CD player

Greeting Ritual

Leader: "Hello, everyone! Let's start our time together by greeting each other!" Ask children to share which skills they practiced since the last meeting. "Before we will continue our adventure, we need to practice attention and impulse control skills."

Clapping Game: Shark

Skills: Attention and interference control

Leader: "Today, we have an exciting trip to the ocean site. But before we will go, we need to practice attention and impulse control skills. We will play the 'Clapping' game again. You have to listen carefully to what I say. When I say the word 'shark,' you will clap. You will not clap if I say something else. So, what do you need to do? (*Solicit responses from children.*) Are you ready?" (*Say one word per second. If children have difficulties, you may say words at the slower pace. Alternatively, if children do not experience difficulty, you may increase speed.*)

LIST: shark, boat, wave, fish, seaweed, shark, sail, fishing pole, shark, life jacket, pail, sand, crab, shell, shark, shark, rock, turtle, sun, shark, umbrella, compass, shark.

Play the game for 3–4 rounds.

Leader: "Now we are going to play this game in the opposite way. You cannot clap when I say 'shark.' You will clap when I say something else. Are you ready?"

LIST: shark, boat, wave, fish, seaweed, shark, sail, fishing pole, shark, life jacket, pail, sand, crab, shell, shark, shark, rock, turtle, sun, shark, umbrella, compass, shark.

Play 3–4 rounds.

Oral Story Recall

Leader: "When our friends looked at the weather for today, they saw that it was cloudy. Do you remember what we decided to do on a cloudy day? (*Pause.*) That's right! We decided to go fishing! Listen carefully to the following story and try to remember it:

Fish are creatures that live in water. Some fish live in freshwater, while some live in salt water. Fish are covered in scales and breathe underwater through their gills. Fish often do not swim alone. Instead, they swim in large groups, which are called 'schools' of fish.

Now, tell me all that you can remember about the story that was just told to you."

Catching a Fish

Skills: Motor inhibition

Leader: "Now, we are going to learn how to catch a fish. Pretend that you have a fishing rod. Our job will be to move our rod back and forth like this to 'cast' the fishing line, so that it goes into the water. (*Demonstrate a casting motion. Make your hands into fists and stack one on top of the other. Move your hands back, over your shoulder. Then, quickly move your hands in unison forward.*) When I will say, 'Cast your lines,' do just like me." (*Practice movement 2–3 times.*)

"The fish will swim by and bite the bait. When that happens, I will say, 'Reel it in.' You have to hold the handle on the rod and reel in the line." (*Demonstrate a reeling motion. For added dramatic effect, you can move the hand holding the pole back and forth as if you are fighting a fish. Practice reeling motion 2–3 times with a command "Reel it in!"*)

"Now, you have listen very carefully for the commands. Are you ready?" Say:

- "Cast your line." Wait 4 seconds. "Reel it in."
- "Cast your line." Wait 7 seconds. "Reel it in."
- "Cast your line." Wait 2 seconds. "Reel it in."

Continue giving commands with various intervals so children have to pay attention and wait for the command.

Who Caught the Fish?

Skills: Visual selective attention

Materials: Fishing Poles Worksheet 7.1 (one per child); Fishing Poles—Key Worksheet 7.2

Leader: "While we are all on our fishing trip, let's keep an eye out for our fishing lines. Fishing lines can tangle easily. Oh, no! Our friends' fishing lines became tangled! See if you can help them untangle their lines. Take a moment to see which winding path each line should follow. You have to use your attention skills." (*Have the children trace with pencils the paths to the fish at the end of the line. Use the Fishing Poles—Key Worksheet 7.2 to check correct paths.*)

Bumping the Fish

Skills: Emotion regulation

Leader: "Let's hear what happened next. While untangling fishing lines with fish, Jose accidentally bumped Jamal's fish from the fishing line. Jamal became very angry because it was a big fish! What can Jamal do?" (*Discuss options presented below with children.*)

1. Jamal could yell at Jose. What could happen if Jamal yells at Jose? How might Jose respond? How might this affect their friendship?

2. Jamal could take one of Jose's fish and throw it back in the water. How might Jose feel? Will it help to solve the problem?

3. Jamal could walk away angrily. Is this a helpful strategy?

4. Jamal could count to ten and calm down. Is this a helpful strategy?

5. He can express his feelings. (Examples: "When you bumped the fish off of my hook, *I* felt really upset because *I* was looking forward to catching a big fish all day.") What do you think about this strategy?

6. Jamal could practice self-talk. (Examples: "I feel angry now. I really wanted that fish. It was just an accident; Jose did not do it on purpose. I want the rest of the day to go better.") Is this a helpful strategy?

Ask volunteers to play Jose and Jamal. Ask Jamal to pretend that he bumped the fish. Encourage a child who acts as Jose to use adaptive strategies to resolve this conflict.

Find Five Differences

Skills: Selective attention

Materials: Find Five Differences Worksheet 7.3 (one per child); Find Five Differences—Key Worksheet 7.4

Leader: "After Jamal and Jose resolve their disagreement, they all begin looking at the fish that were caught. (*Present Find Five Differences Worksheet 7.3.*) At first, both fish may look alike, but they have slight differences. Pay attention to details." Ask the children to begin looking at the fish section by section (e.g., look at the head, then the fins, then the body, and finally at the tail).

Mindfulness on the Beach

Materials: Soft Waves CD Track 7 (5 minutes); CD player

Leader: "In the evening, our friends decided to do a relaxation activity. We're going to join them. Find a comfortable sitting position. (*Give specific directions, depending on your constraints with space. Use a gentle and quiet voice.*) It is a quiet activity, so I will be the one who is talking. Close your eyes. Take slow deep breaths…in and out…in and out…breathe in and out…Now imagine, you are on a white sandy beach near clear blue water. (*Play the Soft Waves CD Track 7.*) A light breeze gently blows your hair and cools your face. Breathe in and out…in and out…The sand is soft and warm, and the water gently laps onto the beach. Shhhhh shhhhhh shhhhh. Breathe in and out…in and out…in and out…Listen to the sound of the water as is washes onto the shore. Breathe in and out…in and out…Enjoy the warm breeze as you walk on the beach…Breathe in and out…in and out…in and out…You feel safe and relaxed…You hear the sounds of the water washing on the shore. Breathe in and out…in and out…Take a few moments to listen to the soft sounds of the water. Breathe in and out…in and out…in and out…Now, slowly open your eyes."

Reflection

Materials: Self-Evaluation Worksheet 2.3 (one per child)

Ask children to identify one thing they learned in today's session. Guide the discussion based on the skills listed in the self-evaluation worksheet. After the discussion, have each child complete self-evaluation on each skill reviewed. With immature children, review each skill together. Thank everybody for working together and being nice to each other. Ask children to practice skills learned in today's session at home and school.

Saying Goodbye

The group performs the ritual and the children are dismissed.

SESSION 8

On the Beach

Session Materials

- Chairs placed in a circle
- Seashells Worksheets 8.1 and Seashells—Key Worksheet 8.2
- Sailing CD Track 5, Soft Waves CD Track 7, and Boat Horns CD Track 8
- Self-Evaluation Worksheet 2.3
- CD player

Greeting Ritual

Leader: "Hello, everyone! Let's start our time together by greeting each other!" Ask children to share which skills they practiced since the last meeting.

Drumming

Skills: Attention and following directions

Leader: "Are you ready for our trip today? Let's get some energy going!" Show the beat using hands and thighs and ask children to repeat the beat. Then ask the child sitting next to you to show another beat. The group repeats. The next child shows the beat, etc. Keep playing for 3–4 rounds.

Oral Story Recall

Leader: "Today, when our friends looked outside, they saw that it was sunny but not too hot. Hmm...do you remember what we decided to do when it was sunny but not too hot outside? (*Solicit responses from children.*) That's right! We decided to go to the beach!

"Now, listen to the story I am going to tell you very carefully because I will ask you to repeat it.

A beach is a place where the water comes right up to meet the land. A beach is usually made of soft yellow or white sand. Many activities can take place at the beach. Some people like to bring shovels and dig big holes in the sand. Other people make beautiful sand castles. Many people like to swim and play in the waves."

Ask children to repeat the story. If some children have difficulty, provide help.

Sailing

Skills: Auditory working memory, selective attention, and motor control

Materials: Sailing CD Track 5

Leader: "Now, let's start sailing. Remember, when the captain says, 'Tack starboard,' you will need to grab the sails and lean to the right side of the boat like this (*demonstrate bending at the waist and pantomiming grabbing sail line*). When the captain says, 'Tack port,' you will need to grab the sail and bend your body the left side of the boat like this (*demonstrate bending at the waist and pantomiming grabbing sail line*). When the captain says, 'Ready about,' you should stand at attention like this..." (*model to children how to stand up straight with hands by their sides facing forward*). Practice for 2–3 rounds before playing Sailing CD Track 5.

"The winds have picked up, and the captain needs your help sailing the boat through the rough waters! You will need to follow the captain's commands quickly. Listen carefully so that you know what to do. When the captain says a command, do it quickly!"

Counting Shells

Skills: Interference control

Materials: Seashells Worksheets 8.1 and Seashells—Key Worksheets 8.2 (one set per child)

Leader: "When Julia, Jose, and Jamal walked on the beach, they found many interesting shells. Julia really likes some shells. Let's help her to find them. You have to use your attention skills." Present children with first page of Seashell Worksheets 8.1 and ask them to circle a target shell, but to ignore others. Note that the second page of Seashell Worksheets 8.1 has a different target shell. After children finish, present them with the Seashell—Key Worksheets 8.2 and ask them to check their work.

Walking on the Beach

Skills: Motor regulation and working memory

Leader: "Now let's go for a walk on the beach. You have to listen carefully. When I say, 'Walk,' walk in the circle. When I say, 'The sand is hot,' hop on one foot like this (*demonstrate*). When you hear, 'High tide,' hold your hands up like this (*demonstrate arms straight up*). When I say, 'Pirates coming,' you have to sit in the crouched position" (*demonstrate*). Ask children to repeat the instructions and practice the commands. After children remember the commands, have them move in the circle and give them directions in a different order. You may use different voice volumes (loud, quiet, and medium) to make this task more complex.

Wet Towels

Skills: Collaborative problem solving

Leader: "Listen what happened next. Our friends were playing together in the sand, and they did not notice that the water slowly began to rise. It was coming right up to the towels that Jamal left on the sand. Now, the towels became soaking wet! Jamal became very angry. He started yelling at Jose, 'Why did you leave our towels near the water? We do not have dry towels anymore!' Jose became very upset and angry also. He said, 'I did not leave the towels near the water. You did it.' Jamal replied, 'No, I did not.' Julia became anxious; she thought they were going to fight.

It looks like our friends have a couple of problems to solve. The first problem is that Jamal and Jose are arguing about who is to blame for getting the towels all wet. If they do not stop arguing, they might start fighting. Our friends were so busy arguing that they have forgotten about the real problem—they did not have dry towels. What must they do first, in order to solve the problem of the wet towels?" (*Prompt children to generate solutions.*)

"Right, Jamal and Jose should stop arguing and calm down. It does not matter who is to blame for getting the towels wet. They are friends and they have an opportunity to work together, along with Julia, to solve the real problem. What could our friends do to solve the problem of the wet towels?" (*Prompt children to generate solutions.*)

"Listen to what Julia said. She offered to spread the towels on the beach to let them dry in the hot sun. It was a great idea!"

Listening to Boat Horns

Skills: Selective auditory attention

Materials: Boat Horns CD Track 8

Leader: "As we wait for the towels to dry, we take a moment to listen to the sounds at the beach. Listen carefully to all of the sounds, and tell me what you hear." Play the Boat Horns CD Track 8. There are sounds of horns of small and large boats. After the children become familiar with the track, ask them to raise their hand when hearing large-boat horns and touch their knee when hearing small-boat horns.

Mindfulness on the Beach

Materials: Soft Waves CD Track 7 (5 minutes); CD player

Leader: "In the evening, our friends decided to do a relaxation activity. We're going to join them. Find a comfortable sitting position. (*Give specific directions, depending on your constraints with space. Use a gentle and quiet voice.*) It is a quiet activity so I will be the one who is talking. Close your eyes. Take slow deep breath…in and out…in and out…breathe in and out…Now imagine, you are on a white sandy beach near clear blue water. (*Play the Soft Waves CD Track 7.*) A light breeze gently blows your hair and cools your face. Breathe in and out…in and out…The sand is soft and warm, and the water gently laps onto the beach. Shhhhh shhhhhh shhhhh. Breathe in and out…in and out…in and out…Listen to the sound of the water as is washes onto the shore. Breathe in and out…in and out…Enjoy the warm breeze as you walk on the beach…Breathe in and out…in and out…in and out…You feel safe and relaxed…..You hear the sounds of the water washing on the shore. Breathe in and out…in and out…Take a few moments to listen to the soft sounds of the water. Breathe in and out…in and out…in and out…Now, slowly open your eyes."

Reflection

Materials: Self-Evaluation Worksheet 2.3 (one per child)

Ask children to identify one thing they learned in today's session. Guide the discussion based on the skills listed in the self-evaluation worksheet. After the discussion, have each child complete self-evaluation on each skill reviewed. With immature children, review each skill together. Thank everybody for working together and being nice to each other. Ask children to practice skills learned in today's session at home and school.

Saying Goodbye

The group performs the ritual and the children are dismissed.

SESSION 9

Going Snorkeling

Session Materials

- Chairs placed in a circle
- Snorkeling Guessing Game Worksheet 9.1
- Sea Animals Worksheet 9.2
- Stargazing CD Track 6
- Self-Evaluation Worksheet 2.3
- CD player

Greeting Ritual

Leader: "Hello, everyone! Let's start our time together by greeting each other!" Ask children to share which skills they practiced since the last meeting.

Clapping Game: Crab

Skills: Attention and interference control

Leader: "Let's practice our attention and impulse control skills. You have to listen carefully to what I say. When I say the word 'crab,' you will clap. You will not clap if I say something else. Are you ready?" Say one word per second. If children have difficulty, you may slow down. Alternatively, you can go faster if children can perform easily.

   LIST: crab, boat, wave, fish, seaweed, crab, sail, fishing pole, crab, life jacket, pail, sand, crab, shell, crab, crab, rock, turtle, sun, crab, umbrella, compass, crab.

   Play the game for 3–4 rounds.

Leader: "Now we are going to play this game in the opposite way. You cannot clap when I say 'crab.' You will clap when I say something else. Are you ready?"

LIST: crab, boat, wave, fish, seaweed, crab, sail, fishing pole, crab, life jacket, pail, sand, crab, shell, crab, crab, rock, turtle, sun, crab, umbrella, compass, crab.

Play 3–4 rounds.

Oral Story Recall

Leader: "Who remembers what we did last time? That's right! We went to the beach! Today, we are going snorkeling! We will see a reef with colorful fish. In order to see the fish, we will need to swim underwater. Don't worry. We will have important tools that will help us to breathe. Now, listen carefully and remember what we will need to do.

"First, we will wear goggles so that we can see fish swimming. Second, we will each breathe through a small tube, called a snorkel, that we will put into our mouths. The end of the snorkel stays above water and lets air come into our mouths. Third, you cannot go snorkeling by yourself because it may not be safe. So, you have to have somebody with you.

"Please, repeat what you learned about snorkeling." Read the story again if children have difficulty with recall.

Deep Breathing

Leader: "Now, we are going to practice breathing under the water. Deep breathing can help us feel calm and relaxed. If you notice that you feel worried or stressed, deep breathing can help you feel better.

- Sit comfortably.
- Place one hand on your stomach and feel it move in and out with each breath.
- Place both hands on your stomach and focus on your breathing, noticing how your stomach moves in and out.
- Breathe in through your nose and out through your mouth.
- Inhale deeply. Fill your lungs slowly.
- Now, breathe out through your mouth.
- Breathe in, breathe out, breathe in, breathe out, breathe in, breathe out, breathe in, breathe out."

Swimming with Fish

Skills: Motor control

Leader: "Now that we have practiced deep breathing, we can swim under the water. We will see many types of fish while we are snorkeling. Small fish swim quickly, so when I say 'small fish,' you need to swim fast like this (*model a quick freestyle stroke*) to keep up with them! If we see a crab, you will need to swim up like this (*model swimming with a slow, short arm strokes*) because if we scare them they will hide! Finally, if we are lucky, we may spot a sea turtle. If we spot a sea turtle, stay still, like this (*model freezing movement*). So, let's see if you remember the instructions. If I say, 'small fish,' how would you swim? (*Ask children to demonstrate.*) What about 'crab'? (*Ask children to demonstrate.*) And turtle? (*Ask children to demonstrate.*) Now we are ready to swim."

Give the following commands: Small fish (pause for 5 seconds); crab (pause for 7 seconds); small fish (pause for 3 seconds); turtle (pause for 5 seconds). Play several rounds and alternate the commands at various intervals.

Guessing Game

Skills: Selective attention and inhibition

Materials: Snorkeling Guessing Game Worksheet 9.1

Leader: "Together with our friends, we went underwater and we saw many interesting things. Let's look at these pictures. What do you see? (*Ask children to name the pictures. If they do not know names, provide the names.*) Let's play a game. I am going to think about something that is drawn here. You have to listen carefully and when I give you enough clues, you can guess." (*If children do remember names, ask them to point at the picture.*)

1. This animal has fins (*pause*). This animal has fins and stripes (**fish**).

2. This animal has a round body (*pause*). This animal has a round body and tentacles or legs (**octopus**).

3. This animal has a shell (*pause*). This animal has a shell and legs (**sea turtle**).

4. This animal has eyes (*pause*). This animal has eyes and fins (*pause*). This animal has eyes, fins, and very sharp teeth (**shark**).

Sea Animals

Skills: Selective attention

Materials: Sea Animals Worksheet 9.2 (one per child)

Leader: "Our friends took pictures of the sea animals during their snorkeling. However, the pictures got mixed up. Let's help Julia, Jose, and Jamal to sort them out."

Present each child with a worksheet and direct their attention to the target items at the top. Ask children to identify which target animals are presented in the overlaid pictures. Note that the overlaid pictures also contain animals that are not present in the target group.

Jose Disappeared!

Skills: Collaborative problem-solving and emotion regulation

Leader: "Let's see what our three friends have been up to! In the afternoon, Julia made lunch. When she finished, she called to Jamal and Jose to eat. Jamal was standing by the water, watching tiny, colorful fish swim by. He hurried over to Julia. Jose did not come, even when Julia called his name again. Julia and Jamal wondered where he could have been. They searched the beach for any sign of their friend, but he was nowhere to be found! Julia became very anxious. She began to worry that something bad had happened to Jose. Her heart started pounding and her palms became sweaty. Suddenly, Jose showed up with the snorkel. Jamal became very angry. His hands curled up into fists, and his face felt red and hot when he thought about what his friend had done."

Discuss with children the following:

- What do you think made Jamal so angry? (Possible answers: Jose violated the rules; there was danger, and Jamal did not know if they could now trust Jose.)
- What could Jamal do to calm himself down?
- What could he think about to make himself feel better?

"Let's hear about Jose. He was very surprised to learn that his two friends had been anxious and angry. Jamal felt himself grow angry again and yelled at Jose for breaking the rule of not snorkeling alone. He told Jose that he didn't know if he could ever trust him again! That made Jose feel angry too, and he started to yell back at Jamal!"

Discuss with children the following:

- What might happen if they continue to act this way?
- How can we help our friends resolve their conflict?

"That was when Julia felt that she had to stop her friends from fighting. She said, 'We all need to calm down.'" Discuss with children strategies the friends used to calm themselves down.

Mindfulness on the Beach

Materials: Stargazing CD Track 6 (5 minutes); CD player

Leader: "In the evening, our friends again decided to do a relaxation activity. We're going to join them, and we are going to do it too. (*Give specific directions, depending on your constraints with space. Use a gentle and quiet voice.*) Close your eyes. We are going to use our imaginations now. Remember, this is a quiet activity, so only I will be talking. You will be using your ears to listen. Take a deep breath…Breathe in…. and out…in…and out… (*Play the Stargazing track.*) The water is calm and the ship is still. You can hear the water softly lap on the shore. Breathe in…. and out…in…and out…As you look up at the dark sky, you see the first stars appear…. then another…and then another…. and another…Breathe in…. and out…in…and out…The stars twinkle and glow, and you see more and more appear. Breathe in…. and out…in…and out…Notice how some stars shine brightly, while others give off a dim light. You can no longer count the stars, as the clear night sky is filled with them. Breathe in…. and out…in…and out…in…. and out…in…and out…You feel relaxed and enjoy the still night. Breathe in…. and out…in…and out…Now take a deep breath, open your eyes, and stretch. Notice the sense of relaxation that stays with you."

Reflection

Materials: Self-Evaluation Worksheet 2.3 (one per child)

Ask children to identify one thing they learned in today's session. Guide the discussion based on the skills listed in the self-evaluation worksheet. After the discussion, have each child complete self-evaluation on each skill reviewed. With immature children, review each skill together. Thank everybody for working together and being nice to each other. Ask children to practice skills learned in today's session at home and school.

Saying Goodbye

The group performs the ritual and the children are dismissed.

Arctic Excursion—Day 1

Session Materials

- Chairs placed in a circle
- Arctic Map Worksheet 10.1
- Snowflakes # 1 Worksheets 10.2 and Snowflakes # 1—Key Worksheets 10.3
- Sounds of Whales CD Track 9
- Pieces of paper with uneven edges for "ice holes"
- Self-Evaluation Worksheet 2.3
- CD player

Greeting Ritual

Leader: "Hello, everyone! Let's start our time together by greeting each other!" Ask children to share which skills they practiced since the last meeting.

Drumming

Skills: Attention and following directions

Leader: "Are you ready for our trip today? Let's get some energy going!" Show the beat using hands and thighs. The group members repeat the beat. Then ask the child sitting next to you to show another beat. The group repeats. The next child shows the beat, etc. Keep playing for 3–4 rounds.

Yes and No Game

Skills: Attention and interference control

Leader: "Before we set off on our next adventure, let's practice another skill that we will be using today. We are going to play the 'Yes and No' game to train our attention and impulse control skills. I am going to ask you different questions. However, you can answer my questions **only** with a complete sentence. You cannot answer with Yes or No. For example, if I ask you 'Do you like ice cream?' you cannot say 'Yes' or 'No.' Instead, you have to say, 'I like ice cream' or 'I do not like ice cream.' You have to use your attention skills." Proceed with the game directing questions at each child. (*NOTE: The list of questions can be extended.*)

- Do you like pizza?
- Can a polar bear fly?
- Can people walk?
- Do you have toys?
- Is the ocean red?
- Do you like apples?
- Is ice cold?
- Do airplanes drive in water?
- Do deer sit in chairs?
- Is grass green?
- Do you have shoes?

Oral Story Recall

Leader: "Today, we are traveling with our friends to the Arctic. Listen carefully and remember what I am going to say:

The Arctic is a cold place with a lot snow. It also has icebergs and mountains. Ice in the Arctic is a beautiful blue color. Visiting the Arctic is a special type of adventure because it is a challenge. We will be walking through snow and hiking mountains. If we are lucky, we can spot an arctic fox or a polar bear."

Ask children to recall the story. Repeat the story if necessary.

Packing a Backpack

Skills: Time management

Materials: A backpack; various items including boxes, shoes, water bottles, and other items that could fit in a backpack

Leader: "Now, we are going to pack our backpack. You have to work fast but carefully. Make sure that you help each other."

Place items in different places in the room away from a backpack. Select one child to be in charge of packing the backpack. The other children will bring items to the packer. Remind children that they need to work together. Tell the children that they have **one minute** for packing. At the end, discuss how they did, what went well, and what could have been done to be more efficient and cooperative. Switch to allow others to be in charge of packing.

Planning Helicopter Landing

Skills: Collaborative decision making and working memory

Materials: Arctic Map Worksheet 10.1 (one per group)

Leader: "Getting to the Arctic is tricky. Luckily, there is something that we can do! We are all going to take a ride in a helicopter that will fly us over the ocean, rivers, and mountains to the place where we will make our camp. It will be a bumpy ride, but the view from above will be very beautiful.

"Before we get into the helicopter and take off, we're going to have to do some planning. The pilot needs to know where we want to land, and our three friends haven't yet figured that out. We are going to look at this map and try to come up with the best place to land. There are some rules we need to remember:

The pilot cannot land on top of a mountain, but can land near a mountain in order to block the wind. We need to be far away from the wild animals and cannot land on thin ice." Ask the children to repeat the aforementioned landing conditions. Present children with the map. "Let's take a look at this map. Where do you think might be the best area for our helicopter landing? Why might that be the best area?"

Snowflakes

Skills: Interference control

Materials: Snowflakes # 1 Worksheets 10.2 and Snowflakes # 1—Key Worksheets 10.3 (one per child)

Leader: "When Julia, Jose, and Jamal landed, it was snowing. There were several types of snowflakes, and Jamal really liked one type. Let's help him to find it." Present children with worksheets and ask them to circle snowflakes of a particular pattern, but to ignore others. Note that the second page has a different target snowflake. After the children finish, present them with a Key and ask them to check their work.

Listen to Whales

Skills: Selective auditory attention

Materials: Sounds of Whales CD Track 9; CD player

Leader: "Now, for our first adventure, let's try to hear some whales out in the ocean. Listen carefully and raise your hand when you hear whales calling amongst the birds' chatter." Play the Sounds of Whales track.

Crossing a Frozen Lake

Skills: Motor modulation

Materials: Pieces of paper with uneven edges to represent ice holes.

Places "ice holes" on the floor.

Leader: "Oh, we have to cross the lake! It looks mostly frozen, but we have to watch very carefully for holes in the ice. We also have to walk slowly and follow each other's footsteps. So, remember, we have two rules: walk slowly and follow each other's steps. Is everybody ready? Here we go!"

Have children walk slowly in single file, following each other's steps and carefully avoiding "ice holes." If some children start walking fast, warn them that they have to be careful; otherwise they can "fall" into the ice hole.

"Great job, everyone! We successfully crossed the frozen lake! Now that we are all across, it is time to continue hiking on the trail."

Jose Got Cold!

Skills: Collaborative problem solving

Leader: "As we were walking across the lake, Jose saw an arctic fox. He left the trail trying to get closer to the fox. Suddenly, his foot plunged into the water. The water was very cold! Jamal and Julia were very good friends, and they caught Jose. He became very cold and started to cry. Jose was also anxious that his foot would freeze and he would not be able to walk."

Discuss with children:

- What might Jamal and Julia need to do to help Jose?
- What can they say to him?

Ask a volunteer to act like Jose, who is nervous and sad. Prompt other children to provide support to him/her.

Jumping around a Bonfire

Skills: Motor coordination

Leader: "Our friends decided to build a bonfire. Let's help them. (*Pretend that you are gathering wood to build the fire.*) So, let's warm our hands and jump in place to warm up."

Ask children to jump all together with a particular rhythm: for example, three jumps and stop. Provide the rhythm by clapping your hands. Make sure that all children jump in unison.

"Good job! Now Jose feels warm! He thanked his friends for their help. In the evening, they discussed what they learned today. What do you think they talked about?" (*Examples may include "being good friends," "you need to follow rules," etc.*) Ask the children to identify situations when they acted as good friends.

Reflection

Materials: Self-Evaluation Worksheet 2.3 (one per child)

Ask the children to identify one thing they learned in today's session. Guide the discussion based on the skills listed in the self-evaluation worksheet. After the discussion, have each child complete self-evaluation on each skill reviewed. With immature children, review each skill together. Thank everybody for working together and being nice to each other. Ask the children to practice skills learned in today's session at home and school.

Saying Goodbye

The group performs the ritual and the children are dismissed.

Arctic Excursion—Day 2

Session Materials

- Chairs placed in a circle
- Pieces of paper with uneven edges for "ice holes"
- Rope
- Snowflakes # 2 Worksheets 11.1 and Snowflakes # 2—Key Worksheets 11.2
- Sounds of Whales CD Track 9
- Self-Evaluation Worksheet 2.3
- CD player

Greeting Ritual

Leader: "Hello, everyone! Let's start our time together by greeting each other!" Ask the children to share which skills they practiced since the last meeting.

Clapping Game: Ice

Skills: Attention and inhibition control

Leader: "We are going to play the 'Clapping' game. You have to listen carefully to what I say. When I say 'ice,' you will clap. You will not clap if I say something else. Are you ready? Use your attention skills." (*Say one word per second.*)

LIST: ice, seal, polar bear, wind, ice, iceberg, fish, ice, snow, cold, ice, whale, ice, wind, ice, ice, snow, ice, fish, iceberg, ice.

Play the game for 3–4 rounds.

Leader: "Now we are going to play this game in the opposite way. When I say 'ice,' you will not clap. You will clap if I say something else. Are you ready?"

LIST: ice, seal, polar bear, wind, ice, iceberg, fish, ice, snow, cold, ice, whale, ice, wind, ice, ice, snow, ice, fish, iceberg, ice.

Play the game for 3–4 rounds.

Discussion

Leader: "Today, we will continue our trip through the Arctic. Just like last time, we expect to find many interesting things here. We will need to use our eyes when walking across icy spots, especially when they are covered by snow. We will also need to use our ears to listen to the sounds of the Arctic. The Arctic is a place where we get to use all of the skills that we have been working on during our time together." Discuss with the children what skills they will need in the Arctic and why they need those skills.

Listen to Whales

Skills: Selective auditory attention

Materials: Sounds of Whales CD Track 9; CD player

Leader: "Now, we are going to use our ears to listen to whales in the ocean like we did last time. Listen carefully and raise your hand when you hear whales calling amongst birds' chatter."

Crossing a Frozen Lake

Skills: Motor coordination

Materials: Pieces of paper with uneven edges to represent ice holes; rope

Provide children with the rope and ask each child to hold on to it (like mountain climbers).

Leader: "It looks like we're going to cross the lake again. This time I will ask you to hold on to this rope and move together. To be extra careful, let's all hold on to this rope as we walk so that if someone slips, they have something to hold on to. Is everybody ready? Here we go!"

Ask children to move slowly and coordinate their movement with each other.

"Great job, everyone! We successfully crossed the frozen lake! Now that we are all across, it is time to continue hiking on the trail."

Snowflakes

Skills: Attention and interference control

Materials: Snowflakes # 2 Worksheets 11.1 and Snowflakes # 2—Key Worksheets 11.2 (one per child)

Leader: "After our friends crossed the lake, it started snowing. There are several types of snowflakes. Two particular snowflakes are among Jamal's favorites. Let's help him to find them." Present children with worksheets and ask them to circle snowflakes of a particular pattern, but to ignore others. Note that the second page has different target snowflakes. After they finish, present them with a Key and ask them to check their work.

Winter Storm Coming

Skills: Emotion regulation

Leader: "As they continued their journey through the Arctic, our friends noticed that the snowfall was getting thicker and the sky became dark. The wind howled. It looked like a storm was coming. The friends were worried about finding a safe place to wait out the storm. Jose felt jittery and afraid. Jamal noticed his heart pounding hard, and Julia felt thoughts racing through her head. They were very anxious! When you feel very anxious, you cannot solve the problem. What can they do to manage their anxiety?" (*Solicit responses from the children.*)

"Let's hear what the friends did. Julia shared with the boys that she felt anxious. Jose felt relieved to hear that he was not the only one feeling anxious. Jamal said that he was also nervous. Sharing feelings with friends helped them to feel less anxious so they could talk about what they could do. Jamal said, 'We need to find a safe place.' Julia quickly spotted a cave. The three found shelter in the cave. They made a bonfire and sat around. Let's join them." (*You may want to sit on the floor and place an object on the floor to represent the bonfire.*)

Collaborative Storytelling

Skills: Listening and inhibition control

Leader: "Jose said, 'Let's tell stories! I can start. Once upon a time, there were three friends. One day…' How can we add to that story? Let's each take a turn." The group leader points to the child sitting next to her/him in the circle and asks to continue the story. The story goes around the circle.

Relaxation/Mindfulness

Leader: "Our friends had a busy day—they need to practice relaxation. We are going to join them. Sit comfortably. Take deep breaths in through your nose and out through your mouth. Breathe in…and out….in and out….Continue to breathe throughout this activity.

Clench your fists in a ball and feel the tension…then release. Breathe in…and out….in and out…Clench your fists again in a ball and feel the tension…release. Now lift your shoulders up as if they could touch your ears. Feel the tension…and release. Breathe in…and out….in and out…Again, lift your shoulders up as if they could touch your ears and feel the tension…Then release…Breathe in…and out…in and out…Tense your thighs by pressing your knees together, as if you were holding a ball between them. Feel the tension….then release…. Breathe in…and out….in and out…Again, tense your thighs by pressing your knees together, as if you were holding a ball between them. Feel the tension…then release…Breathe in…and out….in and out…Breathe in…and out…in…out…in…out."

Reflection

Materials: Self-Evaluation Worksheet 2.3 (one per child)

Ask children to identify one thing they learned in today's session. Guide the discussion based on the skills listed in the self-evaluation worksheet. After the discussion, have each child complete self-evaluation on each skill reviewed. With immature children, review each skill together. Thank everybody for working together and being nice to each other. Ask children to practice skills learned in today's session at home and school.

Saying Goodbye

The group performs the ritual and the children are dismissed.

Going to a Desert—Day 1

Session Materials

- Chairs placed in a circle
- Packing Items Worksheet 12.1
- Snakes Trail Making Worksheet 12.2 and Snakes Trail Making—Key Worksheet 12.3
- Desert Animals Worksheet 12.4
- Snake Rattling CD Track 10 and Stargazing CD Track 6
- Self-Evaluation Worksheet 2.3
- Pencils and crayons
- CD player

Greeting Ritual

Leader: "Hello, everyone! Let's start our time together by greeting each other!" Ask children to share which skills they practiced since the last meeting.

Drumming

Skills: Attention and following directions

Leader: "Are you ready for our trip today? Let's get some energy going!" Show the beat using hands and thighs and ask children to repeat the beat. Then ask the child sitting next to you to show another beat. The group repeats. The next child shows the beat, etc. Keep playing for 3–4 rounds.

Clapping Game: Lizard

Skills: Attention and inhibition control

Leader: "We are going to play the 'Clapping' game. You have to listen carefully to what I say. When I say 'lizard,' you will clap. You will not clap if I say something else. Are you ready?"

LIST: lizard, sand, sun, tarantula, wind, lizard, dunes, cactus, lizard, sand, lizard, sun, heat, lizard, cactus, lizard, lizard, rocks, tarantula, dunes, lizard.

Play the game for 3–4 rounds.

Leader: "Now we are going to play this game in the opposite way. When I say 'lizard' you will not clap. You will not clap if I say something else. Are you ready?"

LIST: lizard, sand, sun, tarantula, wind, lizard, dunes, cactus, lizard, sand, lizard, sun, heat, lizard, cactus, lizard, lizard, rocks, tarantula, dunes, lizard.

Play the game for 3–4 rounds.

Oral Story Recall

Leader: "Today, we are traveling with our friends to Mexico, where we will trek through the Sonoran Desert. Listen carefully about our plans and try to remember what I say.

"Deserts are very hot and dry places where the sun shines brightly. There are mountains of sand called dunes. Not many animals live in the desert because there is very little water for them to drink. However, we will see some birds, reptiles, and lizards.

"What did we learn about the desert so far? What are all of the details that you can remember?" Read the story again if children have difficulty remembering it.

Packing Backpacks for the Desert Trip

Skills: Collaborative planning

Materials: Packing Items Worksheet 12.1 (one per group); backpack outline on poster-size paper; pencils and crayons. (Draw a backpack outline on the paper ahead of time.)

Leader: "We are almost ready to leave for our trip to the Sonoran Desert, but before we go, we need to pack our backpacks with the supplies that we will need. Remember the description of the desert: it is hot, dry, and made up of sand. (*Display the worksheet.*) Now, look at the items that we have here. We cannot bring them all because we will be doing a lot of walking today, and we do not want our backpacks to be too heavy! You can choose only five items. Of these items, which do you think would be the three most important items to bring with us? I will give you one minute to think. Do not shout out your answer before the time expires." Ask children for their choices and write down their answers. Prompt children to discuss the final list and negotiate differences.

Present a large sheet of paper with an outline of a backpack. Prompt each child to decide which one item out of five to draw. Ask children to take turns and draw items in the outline of the backpack.

Snakes Making a Trail

Skills: Selective attention

Materials: Snakes Trail Making Worksheet 12.2 (one per child)

Leader: "Our friends arrived at the desert. Once there, they saw long trails made in the sand. They did not look like footsteps, but instead were thin and long. Jose said, 'I bet these are trails from snakes! Look, there are four different kinds of trails. Let's see if we can pick which snakes made each of these four trails.'" Ask the children to trace the trails using pencils.

Snake Rattling

Skills: Motor inhibition

Materials: Snake Rattling CD Track 10; CD player

Leader: "We just found four different snakes that left trails in the desert. Some of those snakes are harmless, but some are dangerous. We have to be very careful when we walk in the desert so we don't get too close to any rattlesnakes! Rattlesnakes are brown like the sand, so it may be hard to spot them with our eyes. We will use our ears to listen for their rattle sound. If you hear the rattling of a snake, freeze quickly!" (*Play the Snake Ratting CD Track 10.*) Ask the children to move around the circle. When they hear a snake rattling sound, they have to freeze.

Find Desert Animals

Skills: Selective attention

Materials: Desert Animals Worksheet 12.4 (one per child)

Leader: "Our friends took pictures of the desert animals during their trip. However, the pictures got mixed up. Let's help Julia, Jose, and Jamal to sort them out." Present each child with a worksheet and direct their attention to the target items on the top. Ask children to identify which target animals are presented in the overlaid pictures. Note that the overlaid pictures also contain animals that are not present in the target group.

Relaxation/Mindfulness

Materials: Stargazing CD Track 6 (5 minutes); CD player

Leader: "As our friends watched the sun disappear and the desert grow cooler and darker, they also saw the sky come alive with bright, twinkling stars. Julia decided to sit down in the sand and gaze up at the sky. 'Wow,' she said, 'when you're in the desert, the stars look so bright and clear.' Jamal agreed. 'That is because we are in an area that does not have smoke, bright lights, cars, and other sources of pollution. In the desert, the air is pure and clean. That is why, when we are here, we can see many more stars in the sky.' Jose sat down beside Julia and breathed the cool night air. 'It is beautiful,' he said. 'I'm so glad that we visited the desert today.'

"Make yourself comfortable. (*Give specific directions, depending on your constraints with space. Use a gentle and quiet voice.*) Close your eyes. We are going to use our imaginations now. Remember, this is a quiet activity, so only I will be talking. You will be using your ears to listen. Take a deep breath…Breathe in…. and out…in…and out…(*Play the Stargazing track.*) Breathe in…. and out…in…and out…As you look up at the dark sky, you see the first stars appear…. then another…and then another…. and another…Breathe in…. and out…in…and out…The stars twinkle and glow, and you see more and more appear. Breathe in…. and out…in…and out. Notice how some stars shine brightly, while others give off a dim light. You can no longer count the stars, as the clear night sky is filled with them. Breathe in…. and out…in…and out…in…. and out…in…and out…You feel relaxed and enjoy the still night. Breathe in…. and out…in…and out…Now take a deep breath, open your eyes, and stretch. Notice the sense of relaxation that stays with you."

Reflection

Materials: Self-Evaluation Worksheet 2.3 (one per child)

Ask children to identify one thing they learned in today's session. Guide the discussion based on the skills listed in the self-evaluation worksheet. After the discussion, have each child complete self-evaluation on each skill reviewed. With immature children, review each skill together. Thank everybody for working together and being nice to each other. Ask children to practice skills learned in today's session at home and school.

Saying Goodbye

The group performs the ritual and the children are dismissed.

Going to a Desert—Day 2

Session Materials

- Chairs placed in a circle
- Find Seven Differences in the Desert Worksheet 13.1 and Find Seven Differences in the Desert—Key Worksheet 13.2
- Pot Puzzle Template 13.3
- Snake Rattling CD Track 10 and Soft Rain CD Track 4
- Self-Evaluation Worksheet 2.3
- CD player

Greeting Ritual

Leader: "Hello, everyone! Let's start our time together by greeting each other!" Ask children to share which skills they practiced since the last meeting.

Clapping Game: Desert Animals

Skills: Attention and inhibition control

Leader: "We are going to play the 'Clapping' game. You have to listen carefully to what I say. When I say 'lizard' or 'tarantula,' you will clap. You will not clap if I say something else. Are you ready?"

LIST: lizard, sand, sun, tarantula, lizard, wind, lizard, dunes, cactus, tarantula, desert, sand, lizard, sun, heat, cactus, lizard, lizard, rocks, tarantula, dunes, tarantula.

Play the game for 3–4 rounds.

Leader: "Now we are going to play this game in the opposite way. When I say 'lizard' or 'tarantula,' you will not clap. You will only clap when I say something else. Are you ready?"

LIST: lizard, sand, sun, tarantula, lizard, wind, lizard, dunes, cactus, tarantula, desert, sand, lizard, sun, heat, cactus, lizard, lizard, rocks, tarantula, dunes, tarantula.

Play the game for 3–4 rounds.

Comparing Pictures

Skills: Selective visual attention

Materials: Find Seven Differences in the Desert Worksheet 13.1 and Find Seven Differences in the Desert—Key Worksheet 13.2 (one per child)

Leader: "Remember what happened to our friends last time? Where did they go? (*pause*) Right, they went to the Sonoran Desert. On the second day, they continued their trek through the desert. They have refilled their backpacks with the supplies that they need, including containers of water because, as we learned, the desert is a very hot and dry place. While walking through the desert, Jose suddenly said, 'Hey! I think this is the place where my aunt took a picture, but it looks a little different now. I wonder how many things have changed here in ten years?' Jose took the picture from his backpack, and his friends start helping him look for differences. Let's help our friends to find those differences."

Present children with worksheets and ask them to find differences between the two pictures. The Find Seven Differences in the Desert—Key Worksheet 13.2 shows the seven differences.

Snake Rattling

Skills: Motor inhibition

Materials: Snake Rattling CD Track 10; 10–15 small objects representing rocks (e.g., paper clips)

Leader: "Our friends found a place with many interesting rocks. They decided to collect them to bring home. Jose suddenly exclaimed, 'Oh, remember, we have to be very careful because there are some rattlesnakes!' Let's help our friends to collect rocks. So, if you hear the rattling of a snake, freeze quickly!"

Place "rocks" in different locations on the floor. Play the Snake Rattling CD Track 10. Prompt children to collect "rocks" but freeze if they hear a rattling sound.

Going on an Archeological Dig

Skills: Collaborative puzzle making

Materials: Pot Puzzle Template 13.3. Cut the picture of the pot into pieces beforehand. Lamination will allow repeated use.

Leader: "We've made it to an archeological dig site! Some ancient tribes used to live in this area, and we may find the remains of some old pots. Work together to put the pieces together to see what is painted on the pot." Prompt children to work together and talk to each other while doing the puzzle.

Shortage of Water

Skills: Collaborative problem solving

Leader: "Our friends continued walking through the desert. Suddenly, Jamal started to feel that he was getting very hot and uncomfortable. He checked his backpack and found that he did not have any water left. He asked if Julia and Jose had any water. Julia said that she does not have any water either. Jose checked his backpack and found a bottle of water. He opened the bottle and passed it to Jamal. Suddenly, the bottle slipped through his hands and fell on the ground. All the water was gone! Jamal became very angry and started yelling at Jose, 'You are so clumsy; we lost water because of you!' Jose yelled also, 'It was my water; I can do with it whatever I want!' They were very close to fighting. Julia said, 'Boys, you need to calm down.'

"How can our friends resolve this problem without arguing? What advice can we give them?" (*Direct children toward answers—explain that it is okay to realize that it is okay to be nervous in such a situation, and to apologize to one another for behaving angrily or being hurtful.*)

"Let's see how our friends solved this problem. Jamal remembered that in order to solve the problem, he first had to calm himself down. He took a deep breath. Once he was calm, he thought to himself, 'Arguing does not help to solve the problem. It might make the problem worse. I feel angry because it is very hot in the desert and I wish that I had some water. Jose did not drop the water on purpose—it was an accident.' Jamal shared with his friends his feelings and thoughts. They were very appreciative. Jose said, 'I am very sorry that I dropped the water bottle. I feel angry at myself.'

Julia replied, 'When we understand our feelings and talk about them with others, we have more control over our feelings. When we are more relaxed, we can better solve our problem.' Jamal and Jose agreed! They remained calm and kept moving until they reached a settlement where local people gave them water and tasty food. They were very grateful! After the meal, the friends decided to rest for a while. The sun was high and it was hot. Jose said, 'I know how we can cool ourselves down. Let's imagine that we are in the rainforest.' It was a great idea!"

Relaxation/Mindfulness

Materials: Soft Rain CD Track 4 (5 minutes); CD player

Leader: "Find a comfortable position. (*Give specific directions, depending on your constraints with space. Use a gentle and quiet voice.*) Close your eyes. We are going to use our imaginations now. Remember the time when we were in the rainforest. You will be using your ears to listen. Take a deep breath…Breathe in…. and out…in…and out…We are going to pretend that we are in the rainforest…(*Play the Soft Rain CD Track 4.*) The dark cloud brought a light rain. Imagine the sound of the rain as each drop lands on the leaves of the forest….Breathe in…and out…in…and out…It is a gentle rain…Hear the rain…Breathe in…and out…in…and out…Now imagine the tickly feeling of the rain on your body as it gently touches your skin…Breathe in…and out…in…and out…Feel the rain…Feel your stomach rise and fall as you slowly breathe in and out…Breathe in…and out…in…and out…Feel the tiny beads of rainwater cool…Breathe in…and out…in…and out…Breathe in…and out…in…and out…Now, take one more deep breath and open your eyes. Feel the sunshine on your face as you stretch your body."

Reflection

Materials: Self-Evaluation Worksheet 2.3 (one per child)

Ask children to identify one thing they learned in today's session. Guide the discussion based on the skills listed in the self-evaluation worksheet. After the discussion, have each child complete self-evaluation on each skill reviewed. Thank everybody for working together and being nice to each other. Ask children to practice skills learned in today's session at home and school.

Saying Goodbye

The group performs the ritual and the children are dismissed.

SESSION 14

Garden Exploration

Session Materials

- Chairs placed in a circle
- Find Five Differences Butterfly Worksheet 14.1 and Find Five Differences Butterfly—Key Worksheet 14.2
- Bouquet #1 Worksheets 14.3, Bouquet #1—Key Worksheets 14.4, Bouquet #2 Worksheets 14.5, and Bouquet #2—Key Worksheets 14.6
- Birds Singing CD Track 11 and Soft Rain CD Track 4
- Pre-made cutouts of flowers (need color paper)
- Planting a Garden Worksheet 14.7
- Planting a Garden Cards 14.8
- Self-Evaluation Worksheet 2.3
- Poster paper
- CD player
- Pencils, glue sticks

Greeting Ritual

Leader: "Hello, everyone! Let's start our time together by greeting each other!" Ask children to share which skills they practiced since the last meeting.

Drumming

Skills: Attention and following directions

Show the beat using hands and thighs and ask children to repeat the beat. Then ask the child sitting next to you to show another beat. The group repeats. The next child shows the beat, etc. Keep playing for 3–4 rounds.

Oral Story Recall

Leader: "Today, we are traveling to a botanical garden. Listen to what I am going to tell you and try to remember it:

"A botanical garden is a place where people grow many different plants. Some plants like shade, some like sun, and some grow in the water. People take care of all of the plants. When we visit, we might also see birds, crawling insects, and butterflies. It is important to respect all living things."

Ask children to recall the story. Repeat the story if children have difficulty with recall.

Clapping Game: Say Colors

Skills: Attention and interference control

Leader: "Now, we are going to play the 'Clapping' game. You have to listen carefully to what I say. When I say the name of a color, you will clap. You will not clap if I say something else. Are you ready?"

LIST: parrot, blue, flower, red, monkey, orange, rain, trees, yellow, orange, moss, canopy, spider, blue, ant, jaguar, leaves, green, caterpillar, red, blue.

Play the game 3–4 rounds.

Leader: "Now we are going to play this game in the opposite way. When I say the name of a color, you will not clap. You will only clap when I say something other than a color. Are you ready?"

LIST: parrot, blue, flower, red, monkey, orange, rain, trees, yellow, orange, moss, canopy, spider, blue, ant, jaguar, leaves, green, caterpillar, red, blue.

Play the game 3–4 rounds.

Find the Differences

Skills: Sustained and selective attention

Materials: Find Five Differences Butterfly Worksheet 14.1 (one per child)

Leader: "Julia, Jose, and Jamal saw many butterflies in the garden. They found two that look similar, but were not exactly the same." Present the picture of the two butterflies and ask the children to find five differences. Guide the children to look at the butterflies section by section (e.g., look at the antennae, then the heads, then the thorax, and finally at the wings. The five differences are shown on Find Five Differences Butterfly—Key Worksheet 14.2).

Walking in the Garden

Skills: Selective attention and motor inhibition

Materials: Birds Singing CD Track 11; pre-made cutouts of flowers (use color paper); CD player

Place flowers on the floor.

   Leader: "Let's walk in the garden; however, we have to be very careful, as we do not want to step on the flowers. We also do not want to disturb birds. When the birds are singing, we can walk; when they stop singing, we have to stop and stay where we are. Are you ready?" Play the Birds Singing CD Track 11, and have children walk in the garden while avoiding flowers.

Collecting Flowers for a Bouquet

Skills: Cancellation

Materials: Bouquet #1 Worksheets 14.3, Bouquet #1—Key Worksheets 14.4, Bouquet #2 Worksheets 14.5, and Bouquet #2—Key Worksheets 14.6

Part 1. One Flower

Leader: "While in the garden, Julia, Jose, and Jamal decide to collect flowers in order to make bouquets for their mothers. There is one particular flower that is Jose's favorite. Let's help him to find it." Present children with Bouquet #1 Worksheets 14.3 and ask them to circle a flower of a particular type but to ignore others. Note that the second page has a different target flower. After they finish, present them with the Bouquet #1—Key Worksheets 14.4 and ask them to check their work.

Part 2. Two Flowers

Leader: "Jamal and Julia also decided to make their bouquets. There is one particular flower they both like, and one they dislike. Let's help them find the flower they like and get rid of the flower they do not like." Present children with Bouquet #2 Worksheets 14.5 and ask them to circle the first flower in the pair and put a line through the second. They should ignore all other flowers. Note what the second page has different target flowers. After they finish, present them with the Bouquet #2—Key Worksheets 14.6 and ask them to check their work.

Planting a Garden

Skills: Collaborative planning

Materials: Planting a Garden Worksheet 14.7; Planting a Garden Cards 14.8 (one set per group)

Leader: "As our three friends walked through the botanical garden, Jose noticed that there were many people there, working together to take care of the plants. People looked very happy! Jose said, 'Wow. Look at all of the people smiling around us. I think that they are happy because they work together. It might be hard work to take care of a garden, but it feels good to share your work with others.' Jamal and Julia agreed with Jose. So, our friends decided to join people in planting the garden."

Present pictures of plants and discuss symbols indicating a favorable environment for the flowers. Three drops—requires plenty of water; two drops—moderate amount of water; one drop—little water; full sun—sun-loving plants; half sun—partial shade; and no sun—full shade. Explain to the children what each symbol means. Present an outline of the garden and ask children to look carefully at the parts of the garden that are full sun, near water, shade, etc. Engage children in a discussion of how they want to plant the plants. Remind them to work together, take turns, and respect each other's ideas. Discuss how the children worked together.

Making a Bouquet

Materials: Poster paper; pre-made flower cutouts that were used in the Walking in the Garden activity; glue sticks

Skills: Collaborative planning and decision-making

Give children poster paper and flower cutouts. Instruct children that they are going to make a bouquet together. Ask them to take one minute to think about how they want to place the flowers. Remind them not to shout out their answers before the time expires. Ask each child to share his/her ideas and help children to come to an agreement regarding how they want to place flowers on the poster paper. After an agreement has been reached, have the children take turns gluing the flowers on the paper.

Relaxation/Mindfulness

Materials: Soft Rain CD Track 4 (5 minutes); CD player

Leader: "Now we have come to a quiet place in the garden. Find a comfortable position. (*Give specific directions, depending on your constraints with space. Use a gentle and quiet voice.*) Close your eyes. We are going to use our imaginations now. Remember, this is a quiet activity, so only I will be talking. You will be using your ears to listen. Take a deep breath. Breathe in…and out…in…and out…We are going to pretend that we are in the garden. A dark cloud brought a light rain. (*Play the Soft Rain CD Track 4 on the CD.*) Imagine the sound of the rain as each drop lands on the leaves of the forest. Breathe in…and out…in…and out…It is a gentle rain…Listen to the rain. Breathe in…and out…in…and out…Now imagine the tickly feeling of the rain on your body as it gently touches your skin. Breathe in…and out…in…and out…Feel the rain. Feel your stomach rise and fall as you slowly breathe in and out. Breathe in…and out…in…and out…Feel the tiny beads of cool rainwater. Breathe in…and out…in…and out…Breathe in…and out…in…and out…Now, take one more deep breath and open your eyes. Feel the sunshine on your face as you stretch your body."

Reflection

Materials: Self-Evaluation Worksheet 2.3 (one per child)

Ask children to identify one thing they learned in today's session. Guide the discussion based on the skills listed in the self-evaluation worksheet. After the discussion, have each child complete self-evaluation on each skill reviewed. With immature children, review each skill together. Thank everybody for working together and being nice to each other. Ask children to practice skills learned in today's session at home and school.

Saying Goodbye

The group performs the ritual and the children are dismissed.

SESSION 15

Climb Kilimanjaro

Session Materials

- Chairs placed in a circle
- Find Animals Worksheet 15.1
- A backpack; various items including boxes, shoes, water bottles, and other items that can fit in a backpack
- Tent Template 15.2; Mountain Outline Template 15.3
- Masking or duct tape
- Plastic cups, water
- Colored pencils or markers
- Poster paper

Greeting Ritual

Leader: "Hello, everyone! Let's start our time together by greeting each other!" Ask children to share which skills they practiced since the last meeting.

Drumming

Skills: Attention and following directions

Leader: "Are you ready for our trip today? Let's get some energy going!" Show the beat using hands and thighs. The group members repeat the beat. Then ask the child sitting next to you to show another beat. The group repeats. The next child shows the beat, etc. Keep playing for 3–4 rounds.

Watch for the Signal

Skills: Attention and inhibition control

Leader: "I am going to ask you different questions. However, you can answer my questions only if I place my hands like this (*make hands like in prayer*)—that will be the signal. If I do not place my hands like that, you cannot answer my question, even if you really want to answer. So, what do you need to do? (*Solicit responses from children.*) All right! Let's start our game." (*Address the following questions to each child in the group and make hand movement quickly after you ask a question. Alternate the questions with which you pair the hand movements*):

- What's your name?
- Do you like ice cream?
- Can dogs fly?
- What color is your shirt?
- Do you have friends?
- Do cats drink milk?
- Do you like playing games?
- What is your teacher's name?

(*This list can be extended.*)

Now, we are going to play this game in the opposite way. I am going to ask you different questions. However, when I place my hands like this (*make hands like in prayer*), you cannot answer my questions. Remember, when I place my hands like this (*make hands like in prayer*)—that will be the signal that tells you *not* to answer this time. Are you ready?"

- What's your name?
- Do you like ice cream?
- Can dogs fly?
- What color is your shirt?
- Do you have friends?
- Do cats drink milk?
- Do you like playing games?
- What is your teacher's name?

Oral Story Recall

Leader: "Today will be our last journey. Our friends have decided to travel to the continent of Africa. Today, we are going to climb the tallest mountain, which is called Mount Kilimanjaro. Let's learn more about Mount Kilimanjaro, so we will be prepared for our trip. So, listen carefully and try to remember what I say.

"Mount Kilimanjaro is located in Africa. It is a tall mountain! In fact, it is the tallest mountain in Africa. At the top, there is snow and ice. It is always cold at the top. The top is also formed by three volcanoes. One is *dormant*: this means that it is sleeping now, but it could erupt at some time in the future.

What do you remember about Mount Kilimanjaro?"

Packing a Backpack

Skills: Time management

Materials: A backpack; various items including boxes, shoes, water bottles, and other items that can fit into a backpack

Leader: "Now, we are going to pack our backpack. You have to work fast but carefully. Make sure that you help each other."

Place items in different places in the room away from a backpack. Select one child to be in charge of packing the backpack. The other children will bring items to the packer. Remind children that they need to work together. Tell children that they have one minute for packing. At the end, discuss how they did, what went well, and what could have been done to be more efficient and cooperative. Switch to allow others to be in charge of packing.

Find Animals

Skills: Selective attention

Materials: Find Animals Worksheet 15.1

Leader: "Our friends arrived at Mount Kilimanjaro. They spotted many animals and took many pictures. But the pictures got mixed up. Let's help Julia, Jose, and Jamal figure out which animals they saw."

Present each child with a Find Animals Worksheet 15.1 and direct their attention to the target items at the top. Ask children to identify which target animals are presented in the overlaid pictures. Note that the overlaid pictures also contain animals that are not present in the target group.

Crossing a Gully

Skills: Motor coordination

Materials: Masking or duct tape, plastic cups, and water

Leader: "Our friends decided to get water to make their lunch—they got so hungry! They found a little stream nearby; however, to get to the stream they had to cross a gully on a log. Julia became very anxious—she said that she could not do it. How can we help her to overcome her anxiety? (*Solicit responses from children.*) Jose and Jamal said, 'We will help you!'"

Place tape on the floor. Have children take turns crossing the "gully," holding a cup of water in each hand. Ask them to use encouraging statements such as "I can do it!"

Setting Up Camp

Materials: Colored pencils or markers, poster paper; Tent Template 15.2 (needs to be cut out); Mountain Outline Template 15.3

Skills: Collaborative planning and decision-making

Copy an outline of the mountains on the poster paper (you can modify or add details). Have two or three copies of tents, depending on the group size.

Leader: "After lunch, the friends decided to set up camp so they could spend a few days there."

Present the children with an outline of mountains. Ask them to take one minute to think about how they want to place tents. Remind them not to shout out their answers before the time expires. Ask each child to share his/her ideas, and help the children come to an agreement regarding how they want to place tents on the poster paper. Practice collaboration and group decision-making skills. After an agreement has been reached, have children take turns and glue tents on the outline. Ask children to develop rules for the campground. Discuss how they worked together.

Reflection

Leader: "After setting up camp, our friends made a bonfire and sat around it. They decided to remember all their trips.

- What do *you* remember about our trips together?
- What was your favorite part?
- What did you learn during our journey?
- Which skills did you practice?
- What do you want tell the group?"

Give each child your feedback about his/her behavior and participation. Give *specific* praise to everybody!

Saying Goodbye

The group performs the ritual and the children are dismissed.

Audio Recordings

Track 1	Boat Rowing	3:00
Track 2	Forest Sounds	5:00
Track 3	Rainforest Animals	3:00
Track 4	Soft Rain	5:00
Track 5	Sailing	3:00
Track 6	Stargazing	5:00
Track 7	Soft Waves	5:00
Track 8	Boat Horns	2:00
Track 9	Sounds of Whales	2:00
Track 10	Snake Rattling	2:00
Track 11	Birds Singing	3:00

Appendix

* We thank Dariia Yehorova and Tim Henderson for their assistance with graphic design.

Camping Items Worksheet 1.1

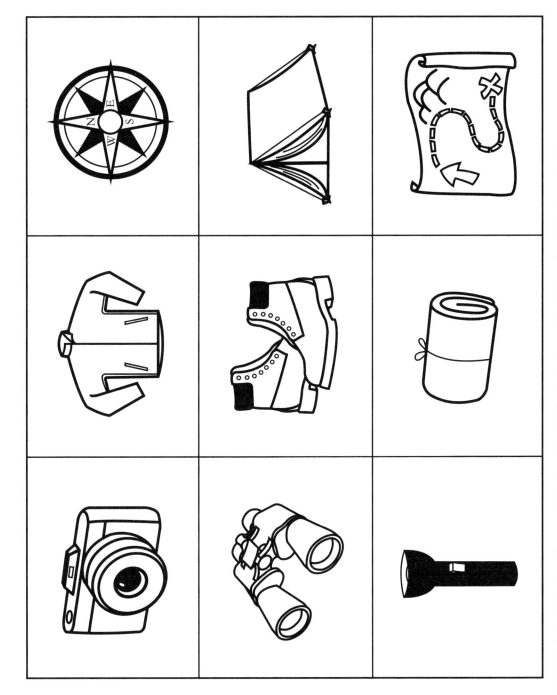

From *Play, Learn, and Enjoy! A Self-Regulation Curriculum for Children*, © 2018 by E.A. Savina, L.M. Anmuth, K.C. Atwood, W.R. Giesing, and V.G. Larsen. Champaign, IL: Research Press (www.researchpress.com, 800-519-2707).

Backpack Outline Worksheet 1.2

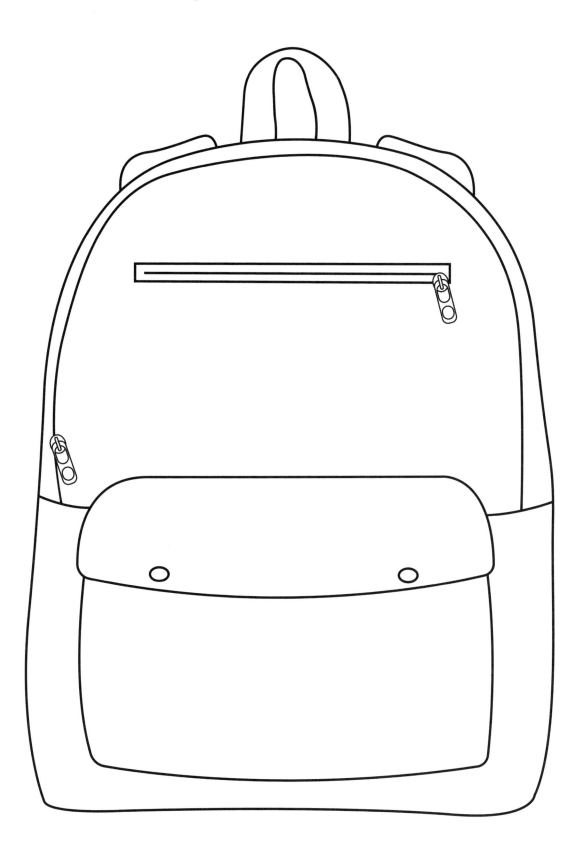

Backpack Items Worksheet 2.1

From *Play, Learn, and Enjoy! A Self-Regulation Curriculum for Children,* © 2018 by E.A. Savina, L.M. Annmuth, K. C. Atwood, W. R. Giesing, and V. G. Larsen. Champaign, IL: Research Press (www.researchpress.com, 800-519-2707).

River Map Worksheet 2.2

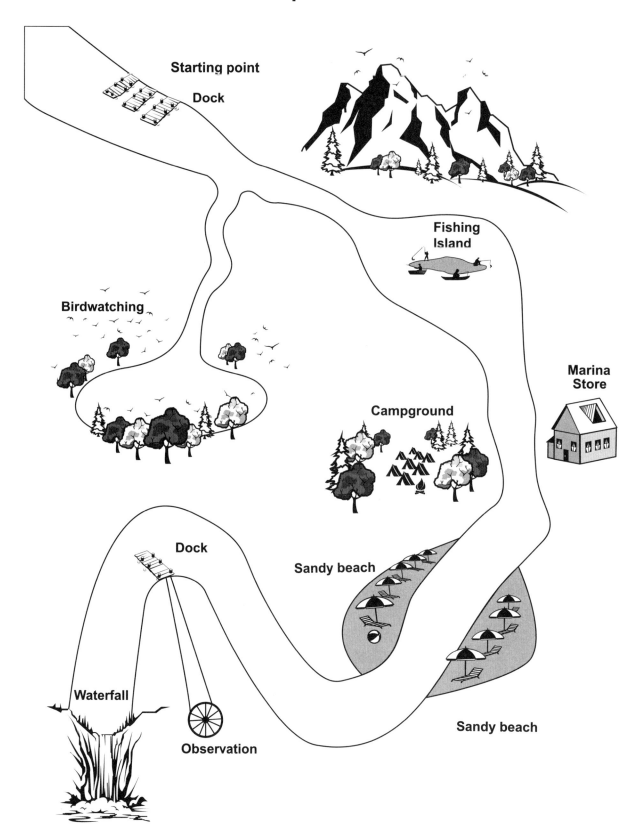

Starting point

Dock

Fishing Island

Birdwatching

Marina Store

Campground

Dock

Sandy beach

Waterfall

Observation

Sandy beach

Self-Evaluation Worksheet 2.3

Name _____   Session _____

	😃	😐	🙁	Did not practice
Attention: I paid attention and ignored things that were not important.				
Impulse Control: I waited my turn and listened to directions. I thought before acting.				
Memory: I remembered stories and directions.				
Emotion Regulation: I controlled my emotions when I was upset, anxious, or angry.				
Relaxation: I could calm down and relax quietly, even after being excited or active.				
Body Control: I controlled my body when doing movement activities.				
Planning: I listened and talked to my peers about a plan before starting an activity.				
Cooperation: I worked with others in a friendly manner. I offered my ideas, but also listened to others.				
Time Management: I did things quickly but without making mistakes.				

😃 **I did well.**   😐 **I did OK. I need some practice.**   🙁 **It was difficult. I need more practice.**

From *Play, Learn, and Enjoy! A Self-Regulation Curriculum for Children,* © 2018 by E.A. Savina, L.M. Anmuth, K.C. Atwood, W.R. Giesing, and V.G. Larsen. Champaign, IL: Research Press (www.researchpress.com, 800-519-2707).

Looking for Animals Worksheet 3.1

From *Play, Learn, and Enjoy! A Self-Regulation Curriculum for Children*, © 2018 by E.A. Savina, L.M. Anmuth, K.C. Atwood, W.R. Giesing, and V.G. Larsen. Champaign, IL: Research Press (www.researchpress.com, 800-519-2707).

Looking for Animals Worksheet 3.2

From *Play, Learn, and Enjoy! A Self-Regulation Curriculum for Children,* © 2018 by E.A. Savina, L.M. Anmuth, K.C. Atwood, W.R. Giesing, and V.G. Larsen. Champaign, IL: Research Press (www.researchpress.com, 800-519-2707).

Looking for Animals Worksheet 3.3

From *Play, Learn, and Enjoy! A Self-Regulation Curriculum for Children,* © 2018 by E.A. Savina, L.M. Anmuth, K.C. Atwood, W.R. Giesing, and V.G. Larsen. Champaign, IL: Research Press (www.researchpress.com, 800-519-2707).

Bird Trail Making Worksheet 3.4

Bird Trail Making — Key Worksheet 3.5

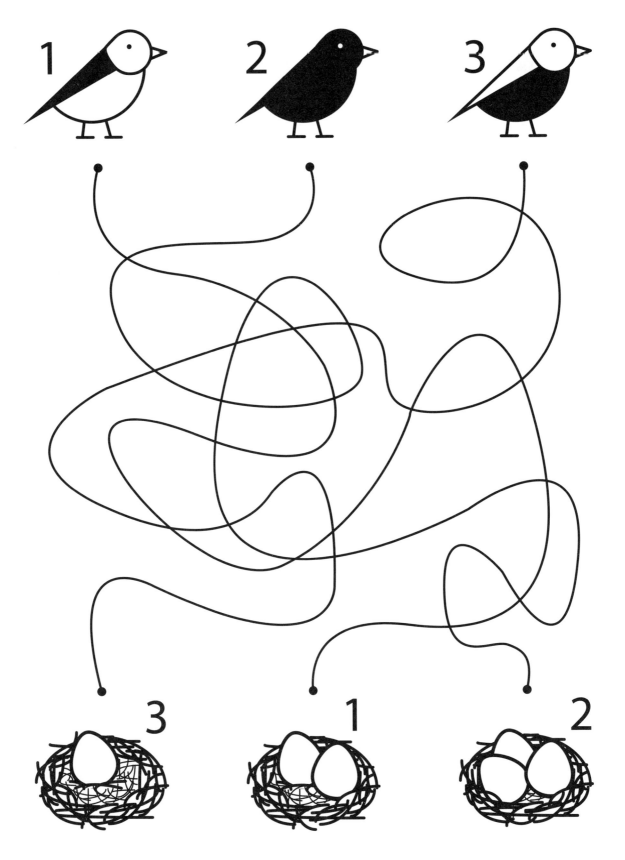

Boat Hole Template 3.6

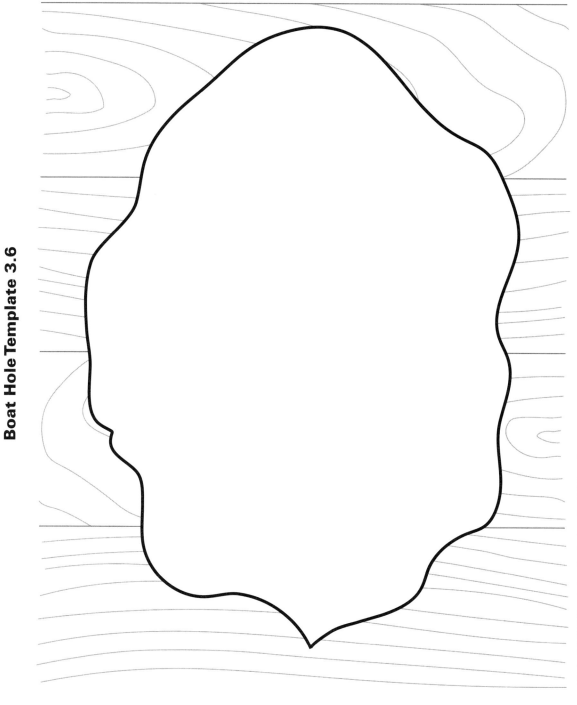

Puzzle Pieces 3.7

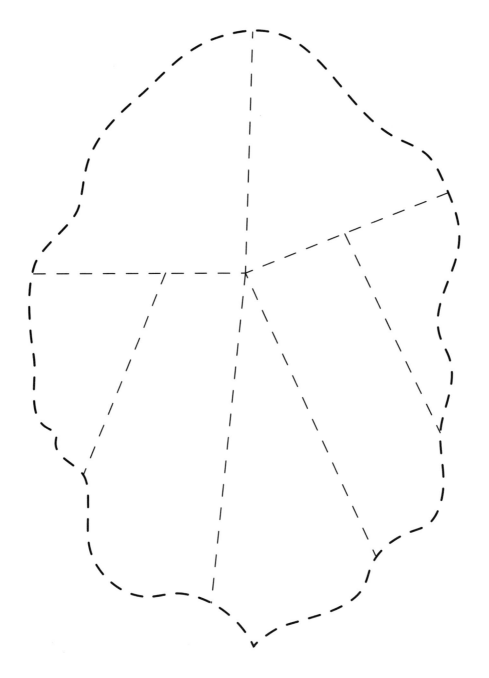

123

Berries #1—Key Worksheets 4.2

Frog Trail Making Worksheet 4.3

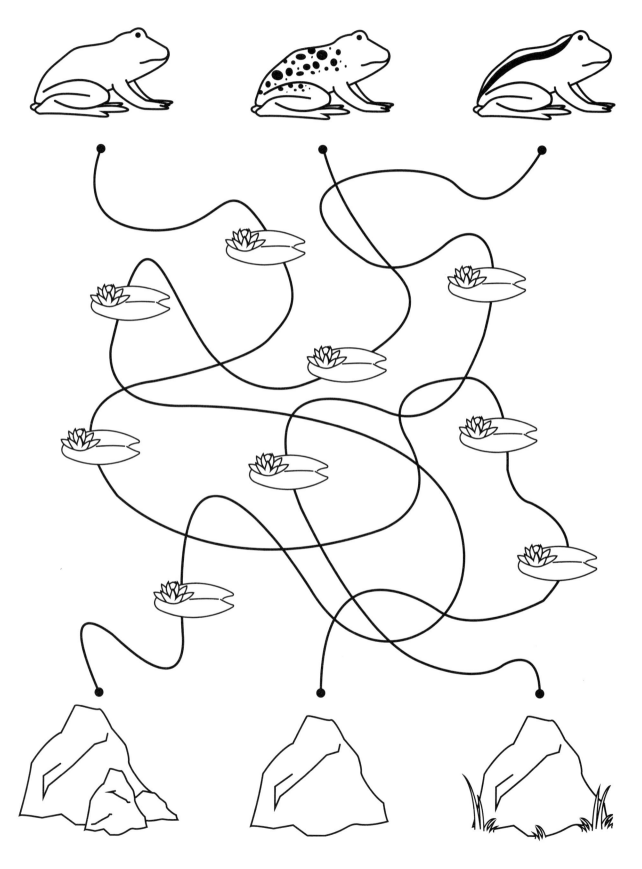

Frog Trail Making—Key Worksheet 4.4

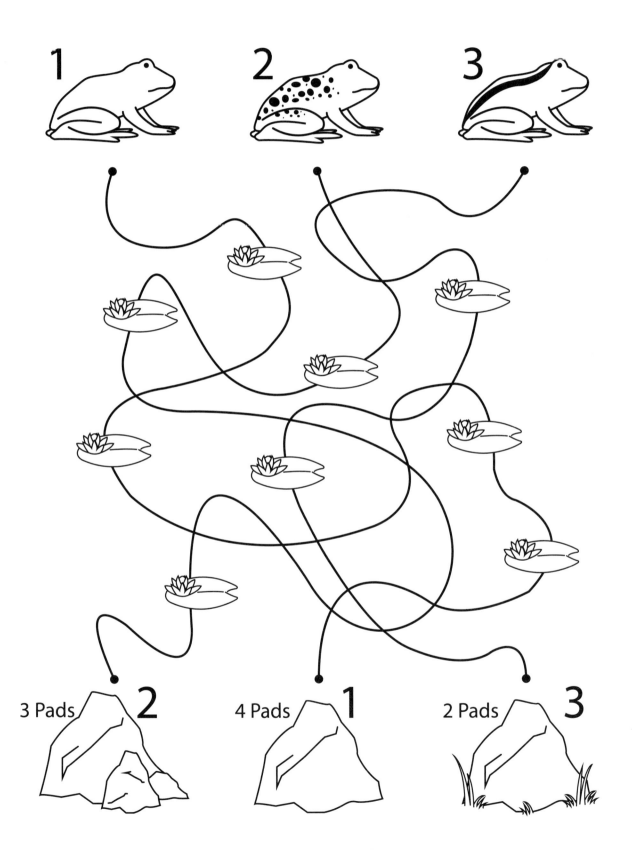

1

2

3

3 Pads 2

4 Pads 1

2 Pads 3

From *Play, Learn, and Enjoy! A Self-Regulation Curriculum for Children*, © 2018 by E.A. Savina, L.M. Anmuth, K.C. Atwood, W.R. Giesing, and V.G. Larsen. Champaign, IL: Research Press (www.researchpress.com, 800-519-2707).

Berries #2 Worksheets 5.2

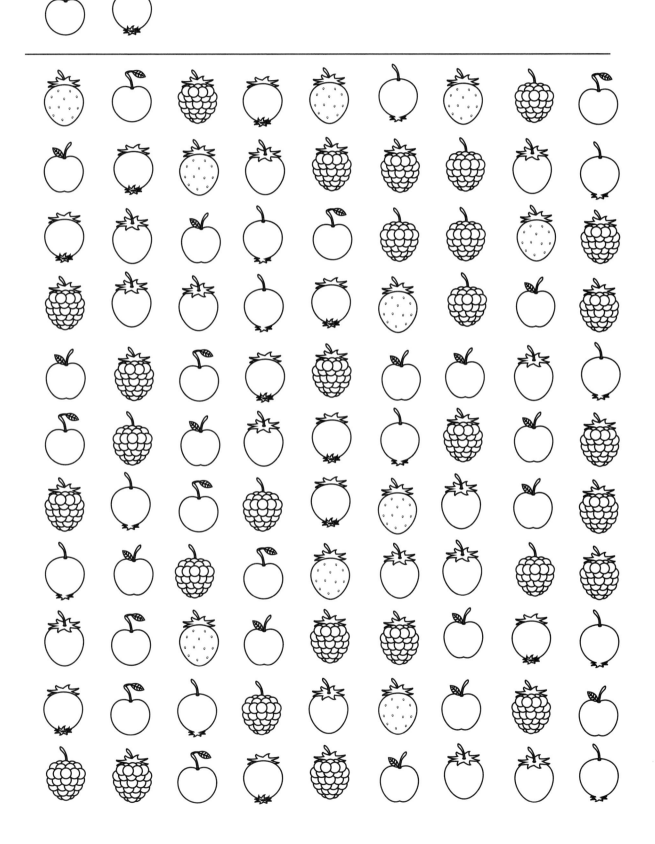

Berries #2—Key Worksheets 5.3

Weather Forecast Worksheet 6.1

Day	Forecast	Trip
1st Day	Cloudy 85 Degress F	
2nd Day	Sunny 80 Degrees F	
3rd Day	Sunny 95 Degrees F	

Islands Map Worksheet 6.2

Beach Island

Fishing Island

Coral Reef Island

Trading Post Items Worksheet 6.3

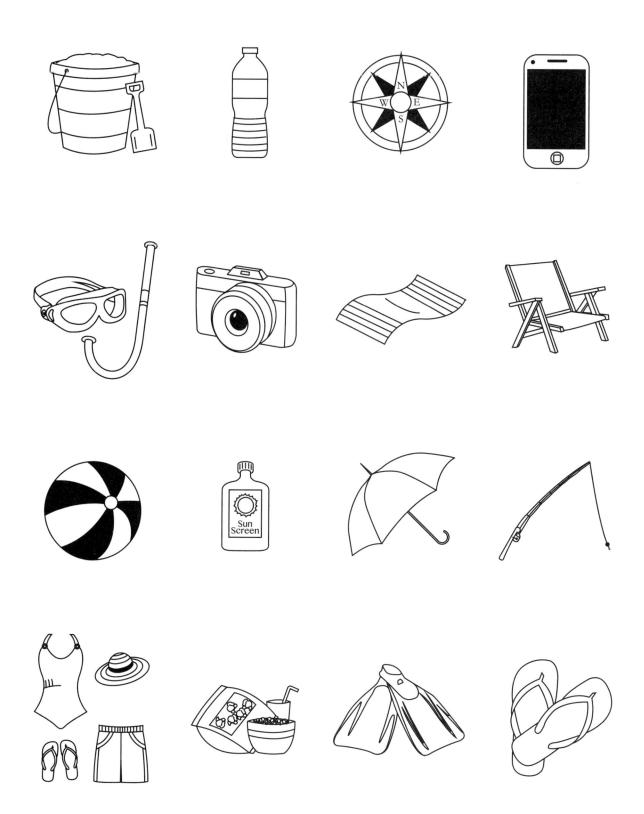

Fishing Poles Worksheet 7.1

Jamal   Jose   Julia

Fishing Poles—Key Worksheet 7.2

Jose   Julia   Jamal

Jamal   Jose   Julia

From *Play, Learn, and Enjoy! A Self-Regulation Curriculum for Children,* © 2018 by E.A. Savina, L.M. Anmuth, K.C. Atwood, W.R. Giesing, and V.G. Larsen. Champaign, IL: Research Press (www.researchpress.com, 800-519-2707).

Find Five Differences Worksheet 7.3

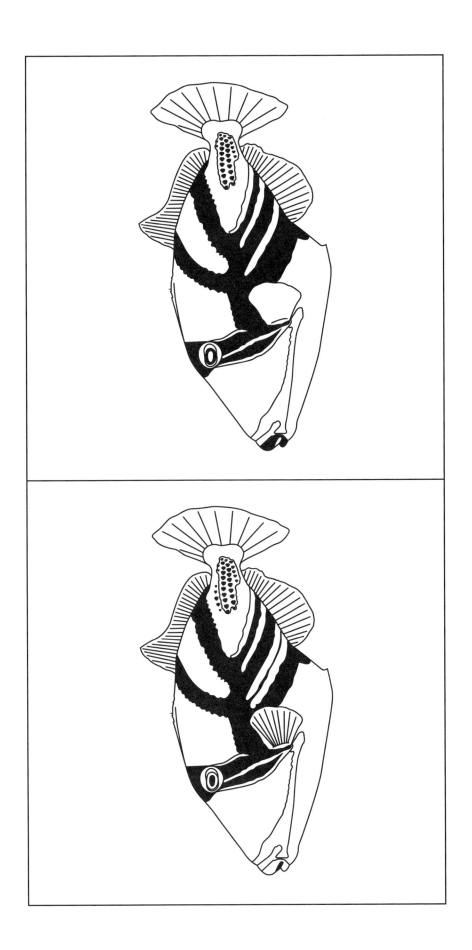

Find Five Differences—Key Worksheet 7.4

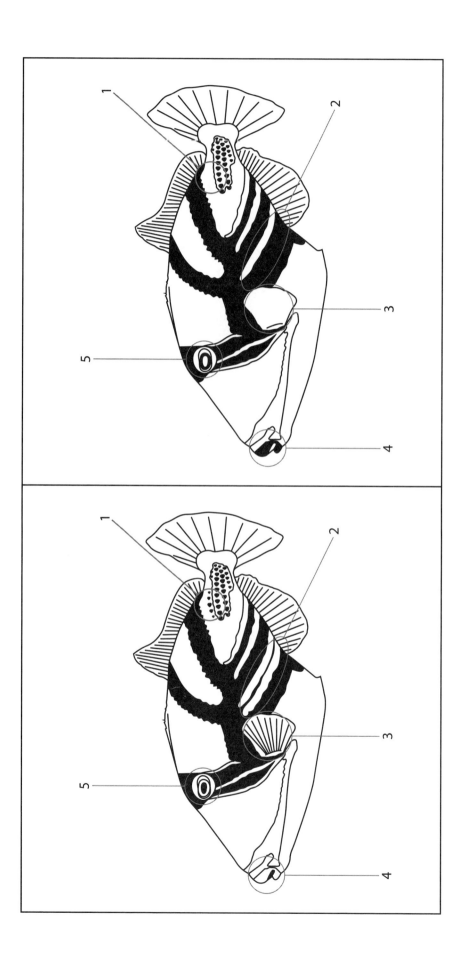

From *Play, Learn, and Enjoy! A Self-Regulation Curriculum for Children*, © 2018 by E.A. Savina, L.M. Anmuth, K.C. Atwood, W.R. Giesing, and V.G. Larsen. Champaign, IL: Research Press (www.researchpress.com, 800-519-2707).

Seashells Worksheets 8.1

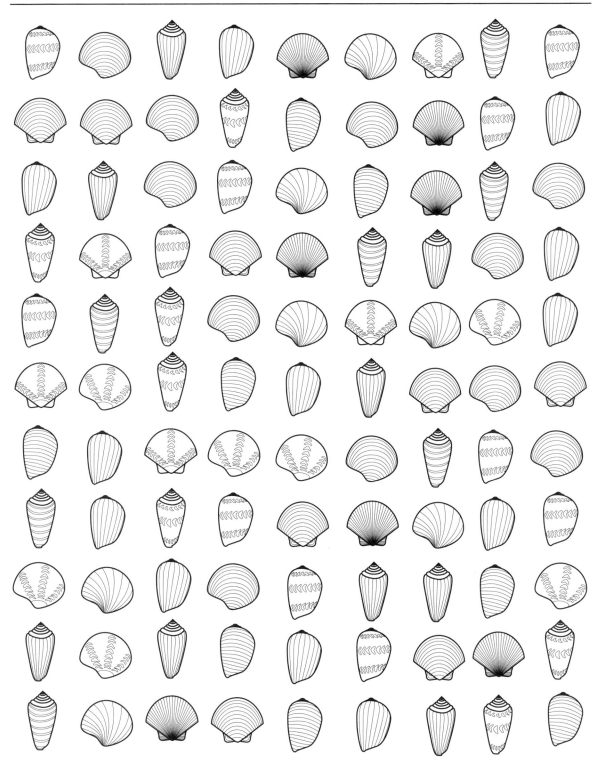

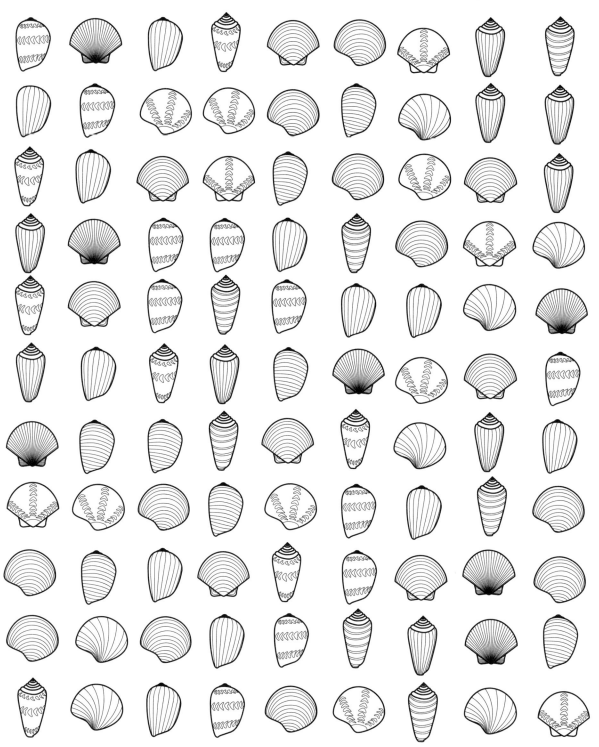

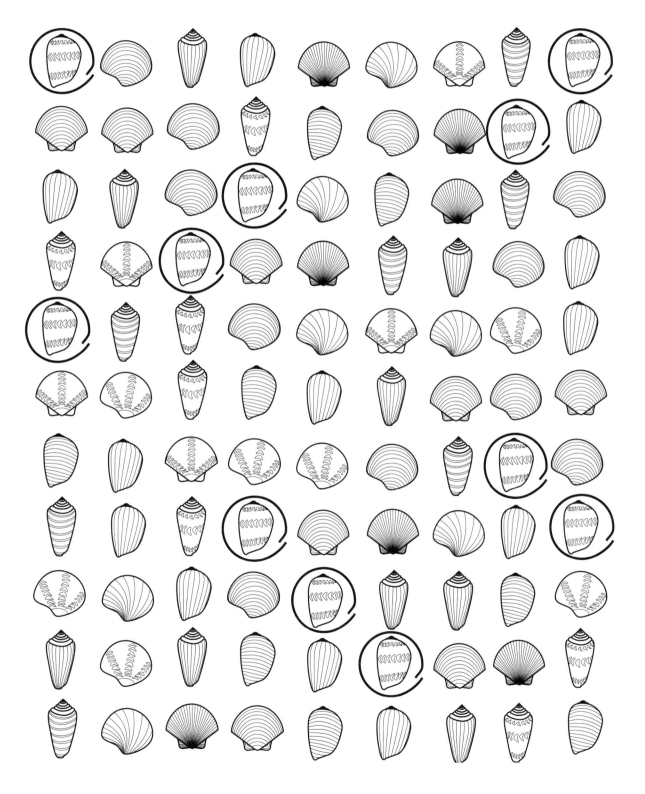

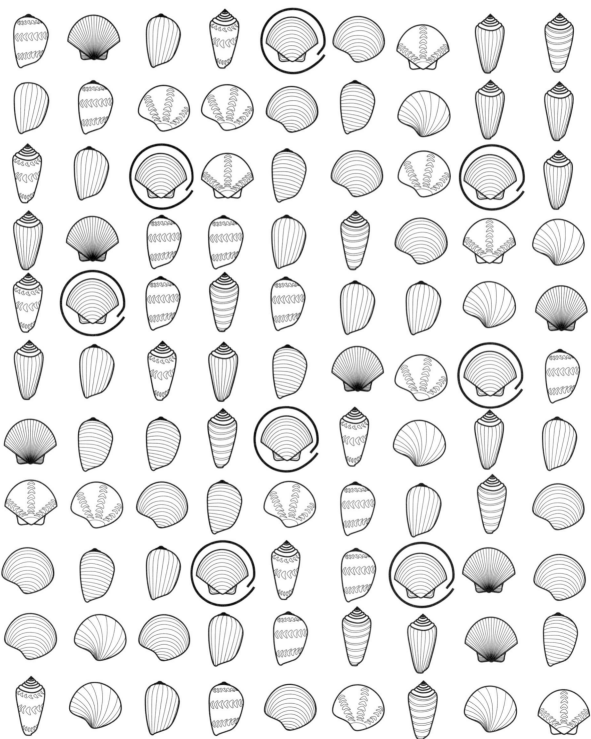

Snorkeling Guessing Game Worksheet 9.1

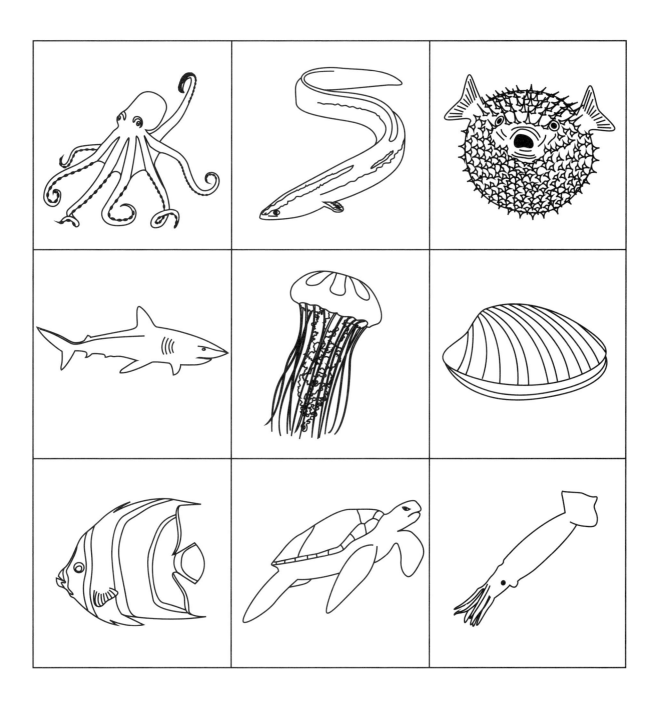

Sea Animals Worksheet 9.2

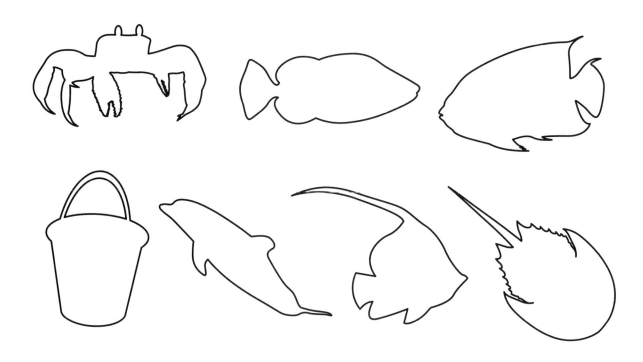

Arctic Map Worksheet 10.1

From *Play, Learn, and Enjoy! A Self-Regulation Curriculum for Children*, © 2018 by E.A. Savina, L.M. Anmuth, K.C. Atwood, W.R. Giesing, and V.G. Larsen. Champaign, IL: Research Press (www.researchpress.com, 800-519-2707).

Snowflakes #1—Key Worksheets 10.3

Snowflakes #2 Worksheets 11.1

From *Play, Learn, and Enjoy! A Self-Regulation Curriculum for Children,* © 2018 by E.A. Savina, L.M. Anmuth, K.C. Atwood,
W.R. Giesing, and V.G. Larsen. Champaign, IL: Research Press (www.researchpress.com, 800-519-2707).

Snowflakes #2—Key Worksheets 11.2

Packing Items Worksheet 12.1

From *Play, Learn, and Enjoy! A Self-Regulation Curriculum for Children,* © 2018 by E.A. Savina, L.M. Anmuth, K.C. Atwood, W.R. Giesing, and V.G. Larsen. Champaign, IL: Research Press (www.researchpress.com, 800-519-2707).

Snakes Trail Making Worksheet 12.2

Desert Animals Worksheet 12.4

Find Seven Differences in the Desert Worksheet 13.1

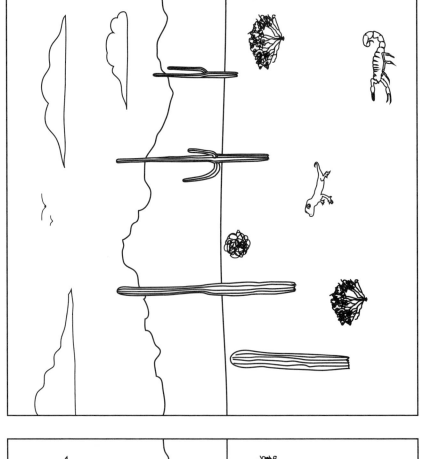

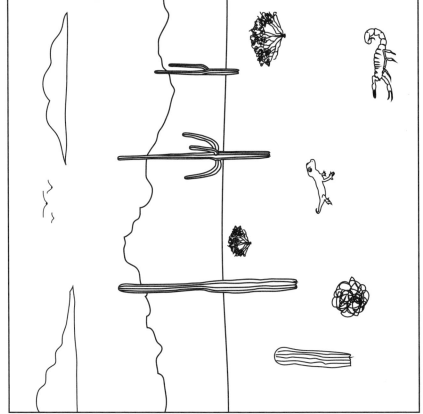

From *Play, Learn, and Enjoy! A Self-Regulation Curriculum for Children,* © 2018 by E.A. Savina, L.M. Anmuth, K.C. Atwood, W.R. Giesing, and V.G. Larsen. Champaign, IL: Research Press (www.researchpress.com, 800-519-2707).

Find Seven Differences in the Desert—Key Worksheet 13.2

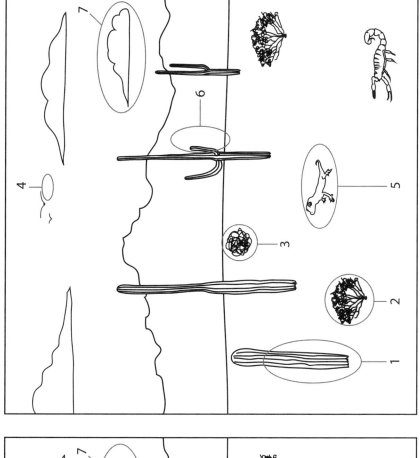

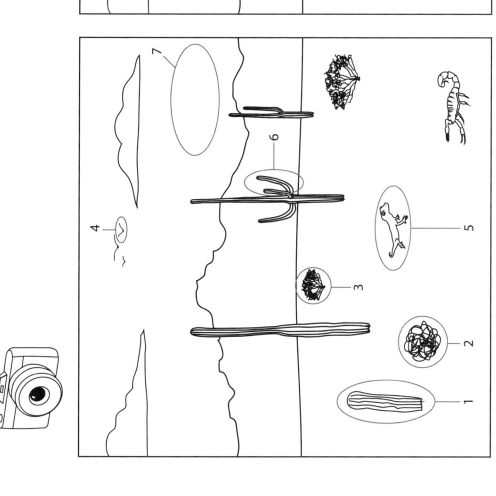

From *Play, Learn, and Enjoy! A Self-Regulation Curriculum for Children*, © 2018 by E.A. Savina, L.M. Anmuth, K.C. Atwood, W.R. Giesing, and V.G. Larsen. Champaign, IL: Research Press (www.researchpress.com, 800-519-2707).

Pot Puzzle Template 13.3

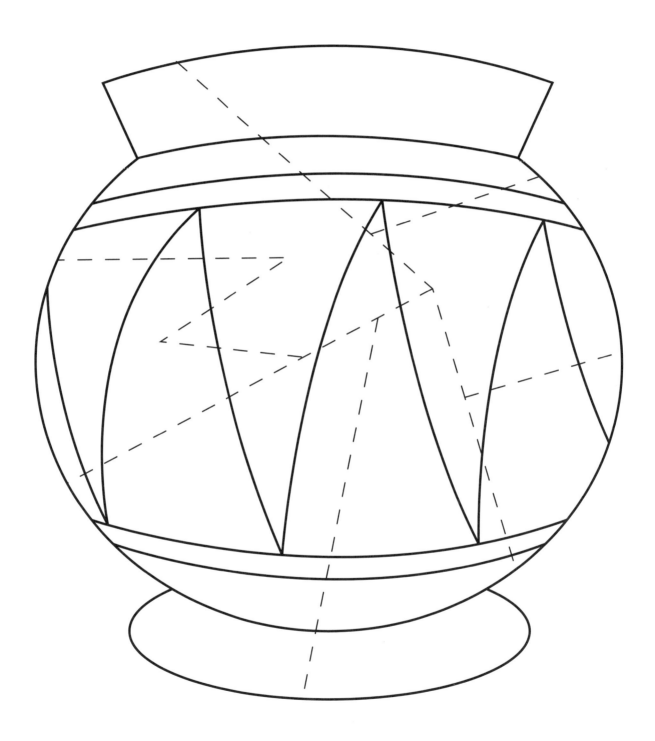

Find Five Differences Butterfly Worksheet 14.1

From *Play, Learn, and Enjoy! A Self-Regulation Curriculum for Children,* © 2018 by E.A. Savina, L.M. Anmuth, K.C. Atwood, W.R. Giesing, and V.G. Larsen. Champaign, IL: Research Press (www.researchpress.com, 800-519-2707).

Find Five Differences Butterfly—Key Worksheet 14.2

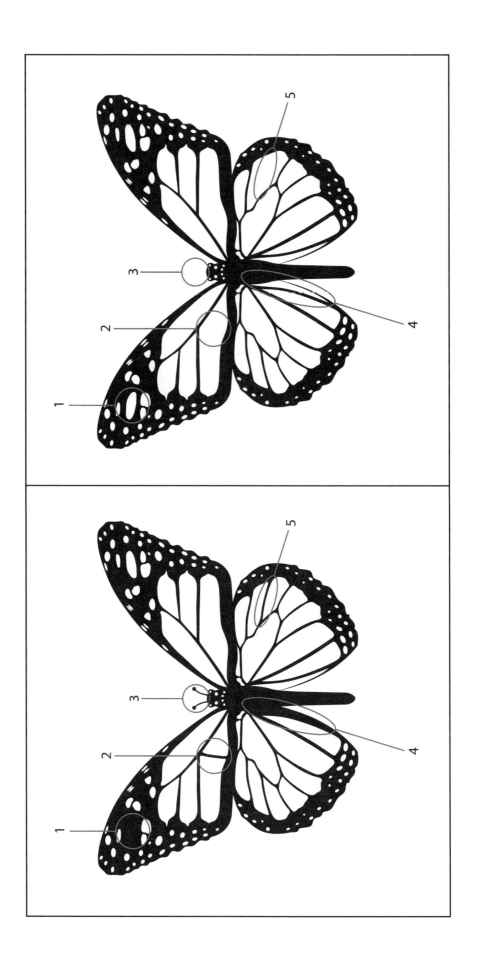

From *Play, Learn, and Enjoy! A Self-Regulation Curriculum for Children,* © 2018 by E.A. Savina, L.M. Anmuth, K.C. Atwood, W.R. Giesing, and V.G. Larsen. Champaign, IL: Research Press (www.researchpress.com, 800-519-2707).

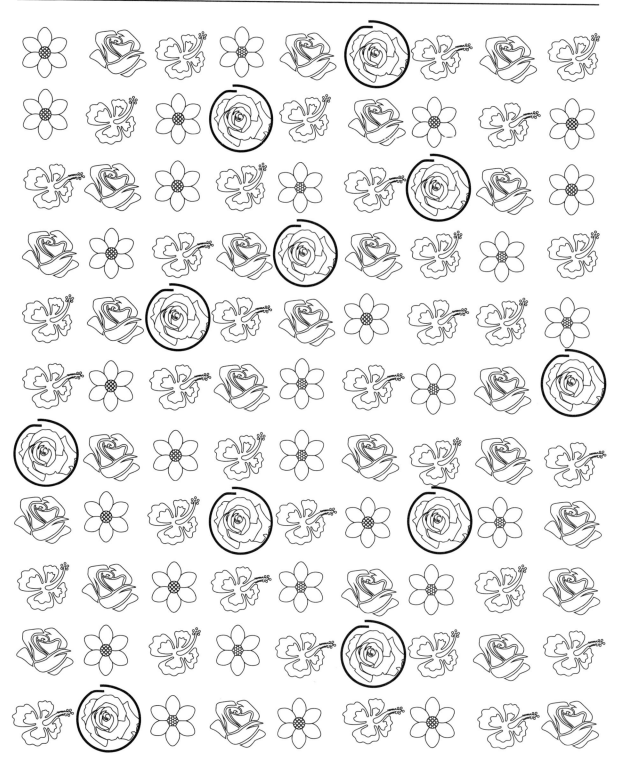

Bouquet #2—Key Worksheets 14.6

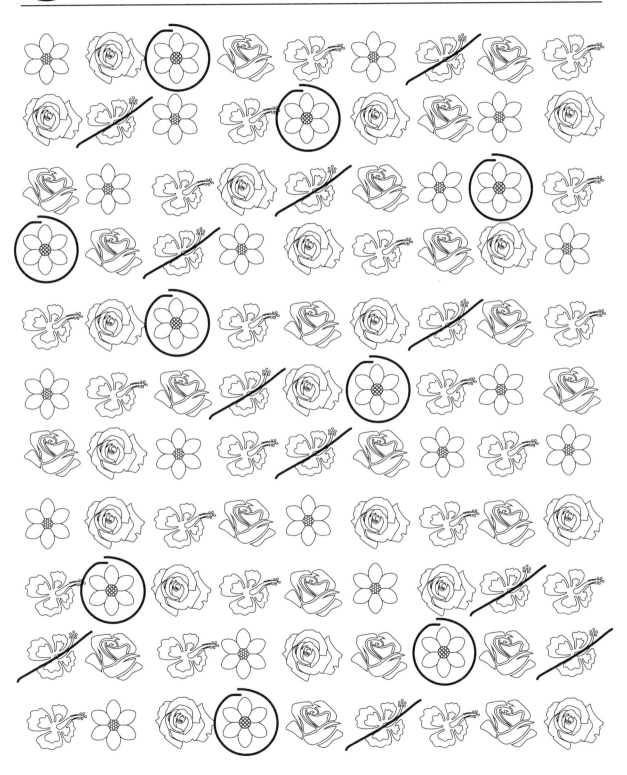

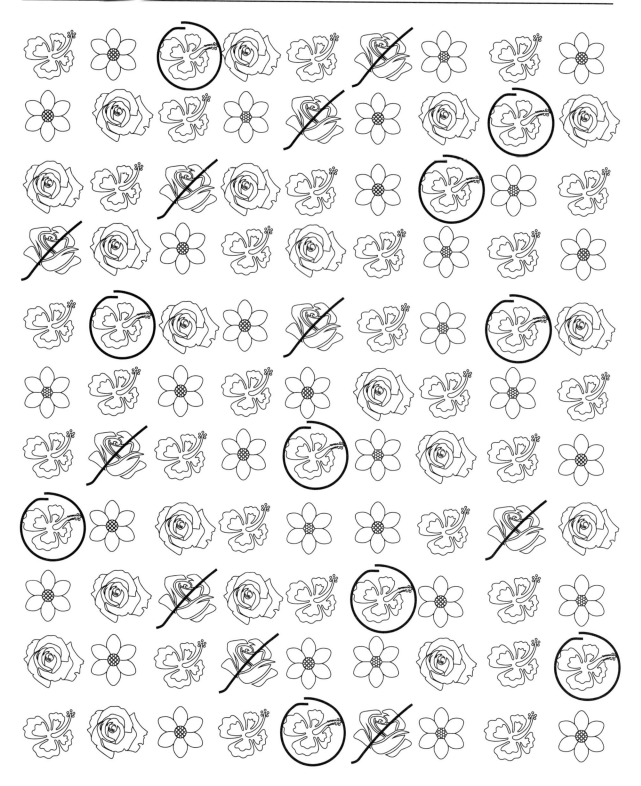

Planting a Garden Worksheet 14.7

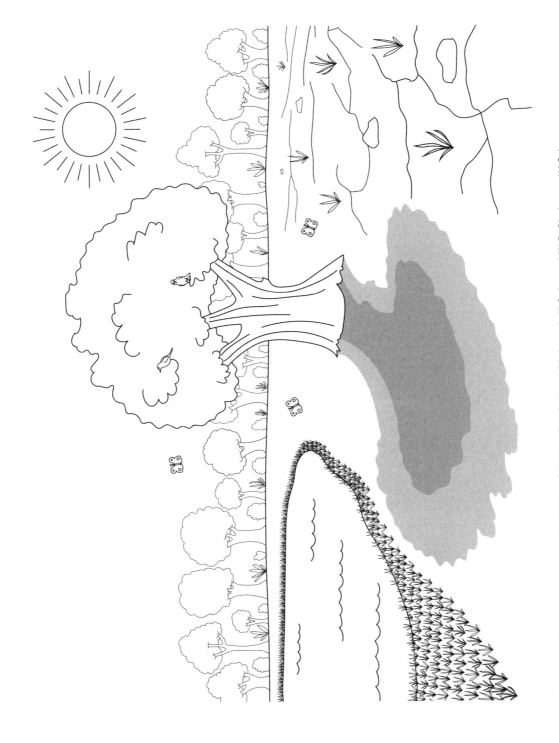

From *Play, Learn, and Enjoy! A Self-Regulation Curriculum for Children*, © 2018 by E.A. Savina, L.M. Anmuth, K.C. Atwood, W.R. Giesing, and V.G. Larsen. Champaign, IL: Research Press (www.researchpress.com, 800-519-2707).

Planting a Garden Cards 14.8

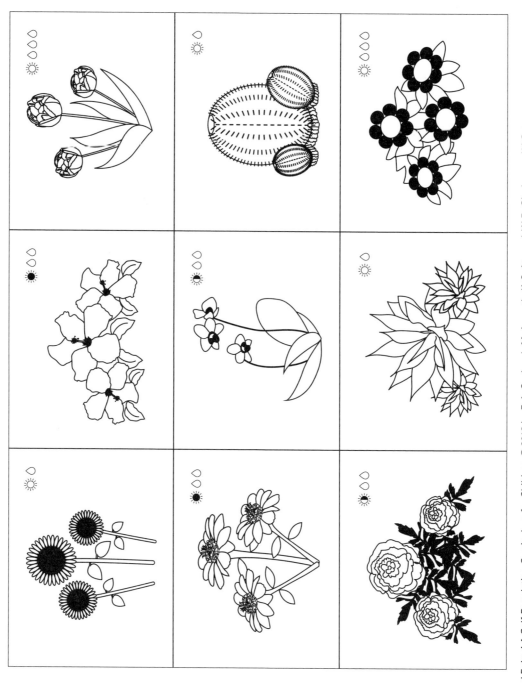

From *Play, Learn, and Enjoy! A Self-Regulation Curriculum for Children*, © 2018 by E.A. Savina, L.M. Annmuth, K.C. Atwood, W.R. Giesing, and V.G. Larsen. Champaign, IL: Research Press (www.researchpress.com, 800-519-2707).

Find Animals Worksheet 15.1

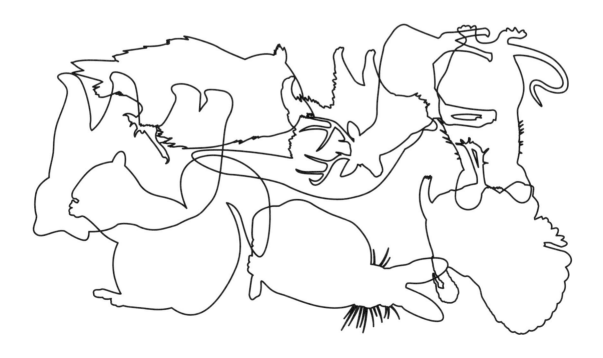

Tent Template 15.2

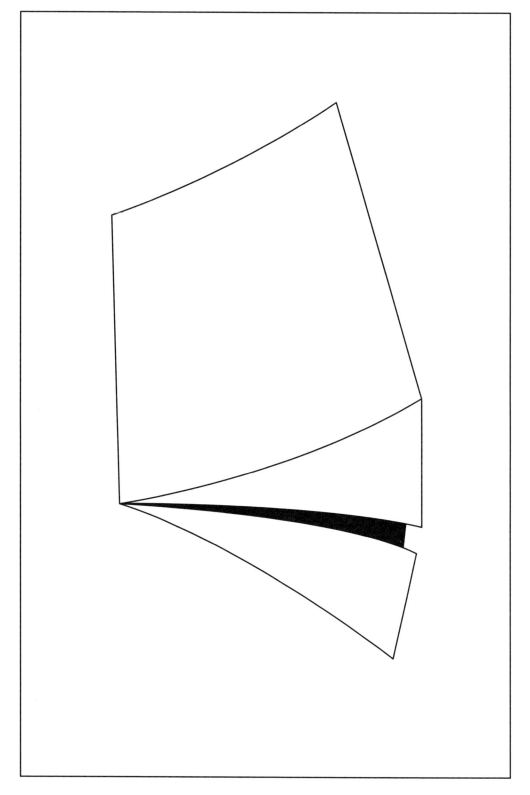

Mountain Outline Template 15.3

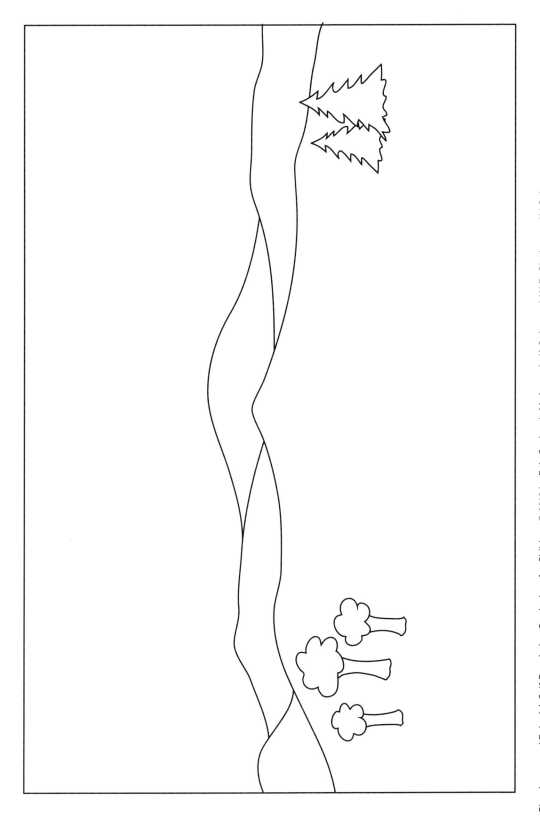

About the Authors

ELENA A. SAVINA received a Ph.D. in Developmental and Educational Psychology from Moscow State Pedagogical University, Russia, and a Ph.D. in School Psychology from the University of Central Arkansas. Presently, she is an associate professor at the Department of Graduate Psychology at James Madison University in Harrisonburg, Virginia. She teaches courses in assessment and supervises clinical practica at the Combined-Integrate Doctoral Program in Clinical and School Psychology. Dr. Savina's research interests include the impact of culture on child socialization and development, and designing programs to promote self-regulation and socio-emotional competencies in children.

LINDSAY M. ANMUTH received a Psy.D. in Combined-Integrated Clinical and School Psychology from James Madison University and an M.A. in Clinical Mental Health Counseling from Rowan University. Currently, she is working as a licensed clinical psychologist in an independent practice in Arlington, Virginia, as well as mentoring LGBT graduate students in psychology. Her research interests have included well-being, systemic and developmental perspectives of distress, and fostering adaptive functioning.

KELLY C. ATWOOD received a Psy.D. in Combined Integrated Clinical and School Psychology from James Madison University. Presently, she is completing a post-doctoral residency in health service psychology at James Madison University and Page Valley Memorial Hospital. Dr. Atwood's research interests include attachment-based interventions and developing programs to promote well-being in children.

WHITNEY R. GIESING received a Psy.D. in Combined Integrated Clinical and School Psychology from James Madison University. She recently completed her predoctoral internship at St. Elizabeths Hospital in Washington, D.C. She resides in New York City. Dr. Giesing's research interests include leadership development, and developing programs to promote self-regulation and socio-emotional competencies in children.

Virginia Gallup Larsen received an M.A. and C.A.G.S in School Psychology and a M.Ed. in Community Agency Counseling from George Mason University. She also holds her national certification in School Psychology (NCSP) and diplomate board certificate in School Neuropsychology from the American Board of School Neuropsychology (ABSNP). Presently, she is a second-year doctoral student in the Department of Graduate Psychology at James Madison University. Ms. Larsen previously served as a School Psychologist for Alexandria City Public Schools in Alexandria, Virginia. Ms. Larsen's research interests include developing programs that promote self-regulation, emotional competencies, and executive functioning in children and adolescents.